NUCLEAR FAMILY

Nuclear Family

UNIVERSITY OF NEW MEXICO PRESS

Ty Bannerman

a memoir of the atomic west

ALBUQUERQUE

Printed in the United States of America

LIBRARY OF CONGRESS CATALOGING-IN-PUBLICATION DATA

NAMES: Bannerman, Ty author

TITLE: Nuclear family : a memoir of the atomic West / Ty Bannerman.

DESCRIPTION: Albuquerque : University of New Mexico Press, 2026.

IDENTIFIERS: LCCN 2025035812 | ISBN 9780826369024 paperback | ISBN 9780826369031 epub

SUBJECTS: LCSH: Nuclear industry—New Mexico—History—20th century | New Mexico—Biography | LCGFT: Biographies

CLASSIFICATION: LCC F796 .B35 2026 | DDC 978.905—dc23/eng/20250808

LC RECORD AVAILABLE AT

https://lccn.loc.gov/2025035812

Founded in 1889, the University of New Mexico sits on the traditional homelands of the Pueblo of Sandia. The original peoples of New Mexico—Pueblo, Navajo, and Apache—since time immemorial have deep connections to the land and have made significant contributions to the broader community statewide. We honor the land itself and those who remain stewards of this land throughout the generations and also acknowledge our committed relationship to Indigenous peoples. We gratefully recognize our history.

COVER ILLUSTRATION by Isaac Morris

DESIGNED BY Isaac Morris

COMPOSED IN Arno Pro and Degular

To my children, Bryce and Bronwyn,

and the world they will live in.

Contents

Preface

Nuclear Family is a history, a history of the everyday, an exploration of how great events seep into normal people's lives and change their courses even as the world changes around them.

My family came to Los Alamos in 1952 to build nuclear bombs. This fact became our origin myth—a fission explosion forms a violent, divine presence looming over the last four generations. And, like any religion, its role in our lives has been argued over, nitpicked, worried, dissected, defended, rejected, and lauded since the day my grandparents first drove up the long, dusty road to the government's secret city in the desert. To be clear, there are no John Smiths of Jamestown among the Bannermans, nor Oppenheimers, standing tall and tortured over the world they created. Just an ordinary family caught in an eddying current beside the whirlpool. Like most families. No one on this planet has been untouched by the nuclear industry and its politics, economy, and science.

So then, here it is, the story of my family, the story of the nuclear bomb, the story of a fallout shelter for schoolchildren, the story of the Incredible Hulk and all the other monsters and heroes of the atomic age, the story of scientists who pushed too far, who died for their cause, who wreaked havoc upon their children; the story of my father, the story of the birth of the universe, the story of a small adobe house on the edge of the Tularosa Basin, where ash fell like snow on a summer day in 1945—all the wonder and violence and life and death of it all—a hybrid beast, a mythical creature drawn upon these pages. A man's head and a dragon's body, a chimera of fire—a family and the world around it.

1

The Beginning

Once the children are settled and the blinds closed, the teacher turns off the classroom lights, gives one more "shh!" for emphasis, then rushes to the projector and switches it on. The screen lights up the room with the familiar countdown sequence, the title card A Is for Atom *appears, and a wobbly fanfare signals the start of the film.*

A mushroom cloud, the rumble of an explosion, and the narrator's paternal, enthusiastic voice announces, "The atomic age was born!"

Pan to a stylized cityscape, all bright colors and akimbo lines. It begins to darken. "There is no denying that since that moment, the shadow of the atom bomb has been across all our lives. All men of goodwill earnestly hope that a realistic control of atomic weapons can and will be achieved. Meanwhile, good sense requires that all of us prepare for any eventuality."

The mushroom cloud again, but this time the smoke pillars upward and resolves itself into a towering human form. "But wisdom demands, too, that we take time to understand this force. Because, here, in fact, is the answer to a dream as old as man himself, a giant of limitless power at man's command.

"And where was it science found that giant? In the atom."

I am forty-three years old, soon to turn forty-four. I am composed of eleven main elements, from oxygen to magnesium, and more than fourteen trace elements like boron, chromium, and vanadium. I wear a beard. I am near-sighted. I am married and have two children; my wife, son, and daughter are composed of the same elements in nearly the same combination as me. In my working life, I write grants to bring food to the hungry, and all of us, grantor, grantee, provider, hungry ones, children, wife, writer, and reader are composed of those same materials. If you were to look closely enough at any of us, you would find the same variety of atoms spinning. And these spinning atoms, or at least their component parts, or at least the energy that created them, have existed since the beginning of time.

In the beginning of time, all of matter, all that ever existed and ever would exist, the proto-pulp of you and me and my children and Julius Robert Oppenheimer and Edward Teller and my grandfather and my grandmother and my wife and Jupiter and Mercury and the sun and every spinning atom of oxygen and magnesium and uranium and every neutron that would go spinning off into the nanoscopic miasma and explosion of fission and, well, *everything*, was crammed together into a single point. And there was no room for discrete particles like atoms then, just undifferentiated matter itself compressed into an infinitesimally, unimaginably small and incredibly, ridiculously, ungodly hot, one-dimensional speck.

And you were there and you were there and you were there.

Was it comfortable? A gauzy excuse for nostalgia? The whole crew together, like a dimly remembered Christmas before all of us went our separate ways?

"It's so good to have us all here," said the matter that would become the Horsehead Nebula to the matter that would become Christopher Columbus. "I hope we can stay in touch."

Or did the heat wear away at all of us, and did we sweat and rustle uncomfortably against each other, the smell of all bodies choking the non-airy void? "Move your goddamned feet," muttered potential carbon to potential Indian Ocean in the hot and stinking dark.

Whatever it was, it didn't last long.

0.0000000000000000000000000000000000000000001 seconds of—and let's remember it this way—the good times. And everyone getting along famously.

Until it exploded.

This is the first of many explosions in the book, so a moment of recognition is due. A buildup of pressure, a sudden welling, a pushing against the boundaries of the nothing that surrounded the something. The universe opened one dilated eye at the precise moment it could take no more, and suddenly . . . existence.

Not light.

Not sound.

Existence itself. It was the biggest and most important explosion in the history of the universe, the event where everything came streaming out of the void. All our bits were born at this moment, so it is fitting that the rest of this story centers on explosions large and small, personal and universal, emotional and historic. Honor the explosions.

The Trinity test, a white light erupting over the desert, turning the sand to glass. Hiroshima. Nagasaki. My parents' birth, another explosion. My own birth, an explosion. My parents fighting, explosion after explosion. The Sedan test, the Rio Blanco shot. My father's death by heart attack, an explosion following an explosion presaging an explosion among explosions all exploding.

But even then, after that first cataclysmic birth, there weren't discrete substances. As the entire universe came streaming and raging out of its single point and spreading outward across space, even then it took thousands of years for the first actual atom to form. The universe had to cool first, and then the tremendous energy resolved into protons, neutrons, and electrons, all whizzing freely, propelled by the still-enormous heat across the eternal explosion of everything.

Imagine us, tumbling in the soupy summation of all as we hurtle toward our own existence. Nothing but moving potential, forming, reforming, unforming, collapsing, building, destroying, living, dying.

As the universe spread outward, it cooled further, and finally, finally the heat had dissipated enough for the protons and electrons to clump. Only then, well after the Beginning, did the first atom, the first in our lineage of existence, the first real member of our family, form.

It was hydrogen. Good old hydrogen. A single proton. A single electron orbiting around it. Followed soon by helium and lithium in great clouds. And then beryllium, boron, carbon, and every single element we know, marching down the steps of the periodic table all the way down, down, down to the heaviest naturally occurring substance: uranium. The last to form, but named for the Greek Titan Uranus, the primordial son of the Earth, and the first Father.

The Beginning was over.

Sometime later (13.7 billion years, give or take a million or so), in a tiny segment of the still-raging explosion of all, in a clump of elements that had resolved themselves into a star system, and on a clump of elements that had resolved themselves into a planet, another clump of elements had somehow pulled off the greatest trick of all, and through processes far too mysterious and complicated to even begin touching upon here, had resolved itself into living, breathing human beings.

But you know that.

And here we are, back at me, forty-three years old, writing grants for a food bank in Albuquerque, New Mexico, the city I was born in because of my family's involvement in atomic science.

Once upon a time, there was a single unit of *me* and a single unit of *you*. One for each of us. An *atomo*, an indivisible unit of being, for every person. A single mote, floating in the black, and quiet only from the outside; a human embryo. Inside, tangles of DNA formed from molecules formed from atoms formed from the indefinable undifferentiable proto-matter at the heart of the Big Bang, the stuff of everything and the stuff of the Beginning. Chemical reactions crackled and coagulated and dripped, forming an entire potential person in a microscopic speck. Ready to explode into being.

My grandfather. My father. My grandmother. My mother. Me.

And then we grew and became wounded and changed according to experience and environment and emotion. The indivisible heart of our being became a forgotten core at the base of a metastasizing identity. Sometimes beautiful, sometimes grotesque, sometimes hateful, sometimes in despair. A bubbling unstable cocktail of influences and manifestations.

2

The First of Us

The Tularosa Basin of New Mexico is a land of emptiness, a desert, a place where water goes to die, where the bubbling comes to an end, a place of nothing. Once it was the bottom of a great sea, but the land is far from the sea now and pulls lost and ragged remnants of water toward it and kills them, spitefully, allowing perhaps for an inch-deep lake to briefly form before evaporating in the blazing nuclear heat of the sun, or draining downward into the utter darkness of brackish underground and unknowable aquifers.

When the Spanish arrived in the late sixteenth century astride their hungry horses, they found only hardship here, slow weakness and the slow loss of life. They named the land Jornada del Muerto. The Journey of the Dead One. It was malpais, badland, worth nothing more than a desperate ride for survival.

And yet.

There *is* life here, somehow. Blue-green lichens upon the rocks, spindly grama grass in the gypsum sands, needle-tipped yucca and cacti squatting on the barren earth, all siphoning the scant moisture from the ground and hungrily consuming energy from the naked beaming rays of the sun, letting the spark of creation pull off another miracle, even here where death should reign. With these miracles paving the way, more miracles follow. Creatures that feed upon the plants: beetles, centipedes, scorpions, pronghorns, and squirrels, all building life from life. Then predatory, killing miracles—mice feeding upon the insects, coyote that stalk waiting for a pronghorn's life to give out, and humans. Native Americans, Spaniards, and Anglo homesteaders have all attempted to form a livelihood in the deathly Tularosa Basin. Many failed. Only a few managed to scratch out a place for themselves in the dirt. But they were here. And they mattered.

Now it is 2019.

I am on the edge of this empty place, in a canyon that digs into the rocky line of hills along the basin's crenelated northeastern boundary. I am walking along a wash that remembers water and longs for its return. It comes down from the steep, sandy hills and tumbles to the bottom, where a dry riverbed awaits it, dust flowing into dust. At a certain point, the slope turns gentle, and there lies a tangle of barbed wire and a pile of rubble that was once a house. I am standing beside it, in the too-bright sun, where a man and a woman named Ratliff lived until the late 1940s.

I've looked for this place before, but I could not find it. That time, I became lost driving down a maze of narrow, nameless dirt roads among the low rises and sudden cliffs that hid along the boundary of hills and canyons. But on this spring day, armed with an old report from the Atomic Energy Commission, I drove slowly, checking the ridges of hills and cliffs and the sloping arroyos that carved troughs between them against the undulating lines on a topographic map. Eventually I found what I was after, a place that was almost like any other in the canyon, a spot that wouldn't warrant a second glance if you were on your way somewhere else. Which you wouldn't be, because there's really nowhere else to go.

Stepping out of the car, I walk among the rubble, shifting stones from a collapsed wall, poking among the litter on the earth. There is broken glass, rusted motor oil cans, half of a door. The remains of lives disappearing into the desert.

I came here to explore these remains. As I enter middle age, I find that there are many absences in my life. People who are gone. Places that, once important, have changed to mean very little to me. A forest in Houston, mowed down and filled with houses; friends who disappeared into their own lives; a sister whom I do not speak to; my father, who died in bed on a Friday morning in April. Holes in the fabric of my understanding of the world.

These absences ache, and the world is full of them, for everyone. We hurtle along the knife edge of the present above an endless chasm of all that is no more. But all these things leave something behind, even if we cannot see it, or don't believe it, or decide it doesn't matter.

On July 15, 1945, the house in this canyon still stood. An adobe dwelling with only two rooms, a pen for livestock behind it, and an outhouse. An elderly couple lived there, Monroe and Minnie Ratliff, as they had since at least 1940. Their twelve-year-old grandson was visiting for the summer. They had a few cows, a number of dogs and goats, all somehow surviving along the edge of death.

Their lives were quiet. Monroe and Minnie had raised seven children, but they were all gone now, departed for various points in the Southwest—California, Texas, other parts of New Mexico. During the days, Monroe and Minnie filled the canyon with their own sounds: quiet conversation, the opening and closing of doors, the bleat of the goats, the bark of the dogs. At night, the low moan of the wind held dominion, or, more often, silence. Their grandson's visit was a welcome new source of sound.

It was Sunday. The Ratliffs were religious, so they spent the day at rest, even though they didn't make the twenty-mile drive through rough country to the nearest church in Carrizozo. Monroe, leather faced and slightly stooped, tended to the cattle and the goats. Minnie, her hair still black but her face furrowed by a life in the sun, fed the dogs. The boy played with the various animals, getting the goat stench all over his hands, but it hardly mattered;

he hadn't bathed in weeks anyway and his black hair stuck out in unkempt cowlicks. After the morning chores and breakfast, the boy ran up into the hills to explore the arid countryside until dinnertime.

At dinner, they ate vegetables from cans, some smoked and salted meat from the last cull. Maybe squash from the kitchen garden.

Then the sun went down behind the canyon walls and the heavy dark of the New Mexico desert nestled around the house. They did not light their lanterns that night, but went to bed when they could no longer see. The few clouds did little to besmirch the thousands and thousands of stars that shone through the small windows in the thick adobe walls.

In the black of the early morning, there was lightning, thunder, and a patter of sudden and forceful rain. The family stirred, wakeful in the storm. The boy left his cot and crawled into his grandparents' iron-framed bed, snuggling his warm body against theirs. He stayed there, even as the storm dissipated and his eyes grew heavy again.

At 5:29 a.m., Monroe swung his bare feet from the bed to the floor and rubbed his eyes.

Through the kitchen window, there was a flash and a glow in the sky to the west. At first, he thought it was the sunrise, but then realized it had come from the wrong direction.

I'm reconstructing these moments. The Ratliffs did not write their story down and they did not leave an oral history of it to their children or grandchildren. All that survives are a few quotes from Monroe in the AEC's report on Trinity and a pile of rubble in a dry New Mexico canyon.

But I want to know their story, I want to be there with them when that flash illuminated the sky. Because in that instant, Monroe saw something that changed the world; it changed me too.

The flash came from a point twenty miles away to the southwest, in the barren Jornada del Muerto. Hours before, scientists, technicians, and soldiers from the Manhattan Project had prepared to detonate the world's first atomic bomb. They had chosen the place because it was wide and flat, close enough to Los Alamos that it could be reached within a few hours' drive, and nearly empty of human population. The closest towns with more than a dozen or so residents were Socorro, fifty-one miles to the northwest, and Carrizozo, nestled in the mountains fifty miles to the east. Other than that, only a few ranchers had homes in the area. Army intelligence agents compiled a list and map of all known persons within a forty-mile radius of the site in case the test explosion wound up releasing enough radiation into the area that it would be necessary to evacuate. But they did not inform those residents as to what would soon happen. There was a war on and secrets to be kept.

In the late-night hours before Monroe put his feet on the dirt floor, a hundred-foot steel tower dominated the staging ground where the test would be held. At its top, a metal shed housed a device the scientists called "the Gadget": a six-foot-diameter steel ball, looped and crisscrossed with cables and wires that connected to explosive charges in its interior. Its heart, a thirteen-pound sphere of plutonium, awaited the moment when its compression would trigger a fission explosion.

Among the bustle of scientists and soldiers was Dr. Louis Hempelmann, a thirty-one-year-old MD with a thick jawline and a high, bony forehead. He had been recruited to the Manhattan Project due to his early experiments with radiation therapy conducted at the University of California, Berkeley; his job in Los Alamos was to determine the harmful effects of plutonium upon the human body, and thus he was a natural choice to lead a team that would determine whether fallout—the cloud of radioactive dust and ash that would rain back down to ground level after the Gadget's detonation—would necessitate medical intervention among the nearby population. A few hours after the test, when the risk of their own exposure was sufficiently low as to keep them from immediate danger, he and five other men on the medical team would take readings at several predetermined points to judge the severity of the effects.

The forecast for July 16 had indicated that the weather would be as close to optimal as possible. However, in the darkness after midnight, distant thunderstorms worried the project leaders, causing the test to be delayed by an hour, until the clouds dissipated.

At 5:29 a.m., J. Robert Oppenheimer gave the signal and detonated the Gadget. A blaze of searing light erupted in purple, then green, then white, as the core of the explosion reached temperatures ten thousand times hotter than the surface of the sun; a rumble of what sounded like thunder, echoed by the nearby hills, reverberated and echoed and reverberated and echoed for endless minutes, seeming to stretch into infinity. The mushroom cloud from the explosion undulated thirty-eight thousand feet upward, flickering like fire and lightning. The broken earth beneath melted and hardened into green glass.

A fireball reached into the clouds like a second sun, roiling and boiling with searing heat. The men of the Manhattan Project, and Frances Dunne, the only woman in attendance, watched it through their nearly black glasses, every one of them holding their breath as it raged across the sky. A human-made miracle as thirteen pounds of metal produced the same energy as a blast of twenty thousand tons of TNT.

And then it was gone.

But it was hardly done. The rumble from that blast would level two cities, precipitate another 2,053 detonations over the next fifty years, simultaneously build tensions and somehow prevent war between two world superpowers, consolidate unprecedented power in the hands of the American president, and create a new and constant source of fear for all the people of the earth.

I imagine that moment, over and over. Maybe we all should. Close your eyes and watch the first nuclear explosion and shudder to think how it shaped your life.

It's personal for me. If it hadn't happened, my grandparents would never have come to New Mexico to be a part of the Los Alamos National Laboratory in the 1950s. My father would not have gone to the University of New Mexico, and he would not have met my mother. And there it is, my existence snuffed out. I would never have come into being, alongside a multitude of others when their families did not move across the country to Los Alamos or Oak Ridge or Hanford or any number of other defense agencies and contractors that were given life by the nuclear age and the Cold War, when their grandfathers did not return from the Pacific theater of World War II or a multitude of hypothetical conflicts that may or may not have erupted in the wake of nonnuclear versions of the US and the USSR.

Everything, everywhere, all of us. Affected forever by this blast in the desert that lasted two minutes, that scintillating ball of flame that passed from golden to purple to green to red in seconds, and then went dark, leaving smoke and ash and radiation behind. An atom or two and our world careens off onto an entirely different path.

At 5:45 a.m., a crew of enlisted men at a position twenty miles northeast from ground zero saw the fallout cloud rising from the explosion site. Ninety minutes after that, a white, ashy powder fell upon their station as the cloud passed overhead. The soldiers were cooking steaks over an open fire, but as the powder began to fall, chemist John Magee shouted for them to put the fires out and bury the meat. The men grumbled, but obeyed.

At 9:40 a.m., Frederic de Hoffman, one of Hempelmann's monitors, arrived at the same station to track the path of the fallout with a Geiger counter. Following a thin dirt road east from the site, he came to a gorge leading into Chupadera Mesa. His counter chattered, then unleashed a barrage of pops, signaling that the area was unusually "hot" with radiation. De Hoffman estimated that the level of gamma radiation (in the "vicinity of 20" rems per hour) approached 90 percent of human tolerance, and was by far the highest recorded outside the ground zero site itself. Since the earlier surveys of human habitation in the area indicated that the canyon was empty of settlement, de Hoffman weighed his options and, realizing that proceeding into it would endanger his own health, wheeled his jeep around and drove back to base.

The fire was blazing in the cast-iron stove as Monroe Ratliff poured himself a cup of coffee from the dented percolator. He drank it down quickly, then pulled on his boots while Minnie cooked breakfast and their grandson stirred among the blankets. With the smell of bacon thick in the air, Monroe opened the wooden door and stepped outside into the cool morning.

He thought, for a moment, that it had snowed. A fine white powder covered the ground around the house, a few flakes blowing in the soft breeze. He took two more steps and reached down to feel the powder. It was warm and crumbled at his touch.

And then what? Perhaps he returned inside, instructing his family to remain indoors for the rest of the day. Or maybe he pragmatically went and fed the animals in their pens before seeing that some had burn marks on their coats.

The Ratliffs, then, were the first of *us*.

Although they did not know it. Although hardly anyone knows them.

The day after Trinity, Dr. Louis Hempelmann, with his lantern jaw and Geiger counter, returned to take readings in the areas de Hoffman had not entered. He and his team drove into the canyon, their jeep kicking up dust as they followed the track of road for about a mile. Then, suddenly, Hempelmann shouted, "Stop!"

Just on a slope in the canyon in front of them was an adobe house. Here, of all places, in the single most radioactive spot other than ground zero itself, a home. Two dogs barked nearby.

He stepped out of the jeep and strode purposefully up to the small house, his shoes leaving prints in the gray-white powder that covered the ground. He knocked at the door. A moment later, it opened and two elderly faces looked up at him. A young boy peered from the shadowy interior.

Hempelmann was shocked, though he didn't show it. Prior to the explosion, the scientists had taken note of every home in the area and removed the handful of people whose ranches and houses they deemed too close to the danger zone. But somehow, the surveyors had missed this canyon entirely. The Ratliffs went unnoticed until this very moment.

The Trinity test was still a secret, and even though Monroe told Hempelmann he had seen the flash of light from the bomb and the white ash falling from the sky and covering the ground like snow, Dr. Hempelmann would not tell them what had happened or why he was there. He looked the family over, saw that they had no burns, that they were not nauseous and that their hair wasn't falling out. It seemed that they had escaped the immediate effects from the fallout, anyway.

Outside, there was still ash on the ground, and some of the animals had singed fur, but the Geiger readings didn't show immediate danger. Hempelmann determined that the walls of the adobe were thick enough to absorb most radiation and decided not to evacuate the family. After thanking Monroe for his time, Hempelmann suggested that he and his family stay indoors for the rest of the day. He shook Monroe's hand, strode back to the jeep, and left.

But the ash continued to fall for three more days. Each morning, the Ratliffs awoke to find the ground and fence posts frosted. In the months to come, radioactive contamination fell upon their home with rainwater and seeped into the ground that their cattle and goats grazed upon.

Hempelmann ordered several more medical assessments of the Ratliffs during the next two years, but they never moved beyond visual analysis, which is to say, a once-over given for sores or visible tumors. Finally, the medical evaluators determined that the Ratliffs had likely not suffered negative effects from the fallout.

Let's talk about radiation for a moment.

Hempelmann and his team were only concerned with the acute effects of radiation poisoning. This is when alpha or beta particles tear into a DNA strand, physically breaking it apart. Molecules go spinning off, blasting into other molecules, creating new, dangerous reactions. Cells die. The body is poisoned, the flesh is burned. The stomach attempts to expel the toxins, resulting in nausea and vomiting. If the damage is extensive, the body's systems are compromised and, well, you die. Nikola Tesla first noted these effects in 1896 when he recorded that his skin turned red and painful after working with X-rays for a prolonged period of time.

These were the signs that Hempelmann and his team were looking for. When he found that the Ratliffs appeared in good health, he assumed that they were more or less in the clear. But high doses of radiation can cause harm in myriad other ways, not by destroying DNA but by changing it. These changes take a number of forms, but all increase the probability that a victim will later in life experience health problems like cancer, genetic damage, and reproductive problems. This type of harm, labeled stochastic, can take up to thirty years to manifest.

Sometime in the intervening years between the Trinity test and the present day, the Ratliffs moved on. No further studies of their well-being were done, and the US government appeared to keep no records on their whereabouts after 1946. I spent many hours trying to track down their history, but the facts I found were ambiguous and isolated. Monroe and Minnie Ratliff had seven children. Monroe died in Tatum, New Mexico, in 1961. Minnie died in Chaves County, New Mexico, in 1986. Some of their children settled in Flagstaff, Arizona.

So, with only a few mentions in papers regarding the Trinity test, they fade, back into the desert, their story illuminated for a brief moment in the light of an atomic blast. The first of us, affected in unknown ways, their presence a mere footnote.

The question lingers in my mind: Why did the government not continue to follow up with the Ratliffs in the years after the Trinity test? Why were they forgotten?

Perhaps Hempelmann did not understand the full ramifications of stochastic harm. However, within the next thirty years, the time frame in which these health effects manifest themselves, the US government had certainly gained a greater understanding of radiation's long-term impact.

For instance, in 1954, following the Castle Bravo nuclear test in the Marshall Islands, the AEC devised a medical treatment and monitoring program called Project 4.1 for the purpose of understanding the short- and long-term effects of radiation exposure to Marshall Islanders who had been caught in the test's fallout cloud.

Early on, Project 4.1 found that the exposure resulted in increased birth defects, miscarriages, and blood-based changes among the population. This convinced the AEC to continue once-yearly medical evaluations of the affected islanders *indefinitely*. Given that this decision was made only nine years after the Trinity test, within the lifetime of the Ratliffs, I wonder why there was no similar effort to follow up with them, or the other ranchers whose livestock and drinking water may have been exposed to Trinity's fallout.

But the answer, I find, is all too clear. Buried in interviews with the original Manhattan Project staff, is Hempelmann's own view of the matter. "A few people were probably overexposed, but they couldn't prove it, and we couldn't prove it," he said in an oral history collected in 1986. "So we just assumed we got away with it."

There it is. Who knows? Who cares? Best to turn away from people who never mattered in the first place. It's expedient.

But I can't shake them. They were exposed to something incredible, horrific, and beyond their understanding. Something that must have changed their quiet, middle-of-nowhere existence in a thousand ways. Something that may have hurt them. And that experience is the same as ours.

So I keep following their trail, scraps of paper and family trees floating on the Internet, social security numbers and emails to people who share their name or are descended from someone who did. I want to know them.

There are signs, shallow footprints they left behind. Names on a census form. Birth certificates. Marriage certificates. Death certificates.

I find out that Monroe was born in Avalon, Texas—a tiny dot on the map with a population of less than a hundred—on July 7, 1887. That Minnie was three years younger, from Allen, Oklahoma—another geographic speck. That Monroe had lived the life of an itinerant worker, that the couple had married in Custer County, Oklahoma, in 1906, when Monroe was nineteen and Minnie sixteen. That they had lived in a place called Goose Creek, Texas, where Monroe worked the wildcat oil fields and where Minnie had their first child.

Shallow footprints, but enough to make me feel a brief flicker of kinship. Goose Creek, later absorbed into Baytown, Texas, was only a few miles from my childhood home on the Gulf Coast. I know what summer is like there. I wonder if the Ratliffs hated it as much as I did.

In my research, I find a handful of relatives living in Hobbs, New Mexico. I contact them and asked about Monroe and Minnie. They have no idea that their family had been involved in this watershed event. They are the children of Lagatha Ratliff, the daughter of Minnie and Monroe. Lagatha died in her twenties, before her children could come to know her well, but they knew of her parents, at least tangentially. They have heard of the homestead in the New Mexico wilderness, which they call "the Goat Ranch." They have a few pictures that they scan and send to me, black-and-white photographs passed down to them.

One is of Lagatha, posing as though she is dancing in front of the canyon house. Another is of Minnie and a grandson, perhaps the same child who stayed with them on the fateful day, tending to the goats in the pasture behind the ranch.

Other than the photographs and a few brief email interactions, though, they don't seem interested in talking to me about their family's role in history.

After a few failed attempts at interviewing them, I give up and leave them to their privacy.

At the ruins of the Ratliff house in the quiet canyon, I hold the photograph of Lagatha in my hand. She is young and full-faced, her hands are on her hips, and she is giving the camera a coquettish smile. Behind her, the old house stands, whole, in place of the rubble that is now before me. A juniper tree is in the foreground, used as a makeshift fence post for a small front yard.

I lower the photograph from my view, and the juniper tree is still there, looking almost the same as it did over seventy years ago. I walk to it. A strand of wire is wrapped around its trunk, the wood growing over it in places. I run my hand along the gnarled bark.

I suppose this is the closest I'll get to understanding their lives. Their trail is so cold now, it is impossible that anyone will ever know exactly how they were affected by the bomb. But isn't that the case for all of us? The effects of that nuclear blast rolled across the whole world and changed everything in ways too diffuse to quantify.

INTERLUDE

The Miracle

Uranus, now, rises again. Father of Titans, he carried a secret inside of him, and Oppenheimer took it. The great secret of the universe: that the atom is breakable and untold energy lies within.

Uranium, the youngest of the naturally occurring elements, waited eons for someone to find its power. In the fifteenth century, Czech miners dug up an amorphous black ore they named "pitchblende." It was useful in coloring glass and porcelain, but its true treasure would remain hidden until 1789, when German chemist Martin Heinrich Klaproth extracted a black powder from the mélange of metals and named it "uranium."

In 1896, French physicist Antoine Henri Becquerel found that a chunk of this metal ruined a nearby photographic plate; he theorized that it must emit some form of invisible light. In 1935, American physicist Arthur Dempster found that one of uranium's isotopes, uranium-235, was unstable enough to shoot out a neutron from time to time. And in 1942, Enrico Fermi and Leo Szilard used U-235 to create the first self-sustaining radioactive chain reaction in a nuclear pile at the University of Chicago.

Uranium's power all comes down to that stray neutron, a subatomic particle that is so unassuming that it doesn't even carry a charge. A lump of U-235 (uranium with 92 protons and 143 neutrons) is unstable, meaning that the forces holding its nucleus together are naturally weak. Every once in a while, at a time of its own choosing beyond our understanding, a neutron will escape from the core and spin off into the unknown. If that unknown happens to be another atom of U-235, then the neutron will enter its orbit, creating the even more unstable atomic isotope of U-236, which then immediately releases three neutrons of its own. And if those neutrons find more U-235? It happens again and again, a chain reaction, each fracturing atom emitting a blast of energy, compounding and compounding into unimaginable searing heat and light.

In 1945, it was up to Oppenheimer to steal the fire at the god's heart. He did. And he paid for it.

3

The Hearing

Once upon a time, my grandmother Bernice was young.

No, this is true.

Her face, now covered in spiraling wrinkles, was smooth. Her skin was not scorched and thin and fragile as rice paper, tearing when she falls on loose gravel in the driveway or sometimes after a brush against a rough plaster patch on the wall. She still wore glasses, but her left eye was not shrunken and blind. Her voice was just as loud and brash as it is now, but she could hear the words of others clearly and did not need the hearing aid that both picks up conversation and makes the clatter of silverware intolerable. Once upon a time, she was not even a grandmother.

Once upon a time, she was twenty-five years old.

My grandfather Dan Bannerman was still alive and strong. My uncle, who stands in the kitchen at my grandmother's house brewing a cup of tea as I ask her about these years, was not yet born. My father, dead now for two decades, was a two-year old child, full of energy and innocent curiosity, as prone to tantrums as any child. The world was still far away from my birth.

And it was 1952, and she and Dan and my two-year old father drove in a 1944 Chrysler convertible from the burgeoning city of Los Angeles into the dry, empty lands of New Mexico. They left behind their families and lives in a city, a real city, where nearly two million people already crowded together, and traveled to the hilltop laboratory of Los Alamos. There, some ten thousand workers, scientists, and their families were building new lives in a town that the government had only created ten years before.

Back in Los Angeles, recruiters from Los Alamos had offered my grandfather a position as an associate scientist at the lab, and he had accepted with the patriotic enthusiasm endemic to the time. He remembered his great relief seven years before when a new kind of bomb, developed in Los Alamos, forced a Japanese surrender and brought about the end of World War II.

At the same time, my grandmother applied for a position tending to animals at the Los Alamos biology lab, and the recruiters told her that she was a shoo-in once her security clearance had been granted. This, even though her educational background was in sociology.

They answered the government's call and they came to the top of the Pajarito Plateau on a dusty, sun-filled day; they showed their paperwork at the chain link gate that surrounded the city and were waved inside the perimeter by the guards beneath the machine-gun towers.

And this is the beginning, right here, as they drive on that dusty road, of my family. I know these people. I know New Mexico. I remember being a child in the pine trees of Los Alamos.

Los Angeles and Michigan and Scotland and France, and all those people who came before, stretching back and back, mean nothing to me. No matter their claims to various slices of my DNA, I never held their hands. But I held my grandmother's hand in the forests of Los Alamos.

Seated at the dining room table across from her as she haltingly talks about her first years in the town, I try to put myself in her place. It was a lonely time for her. My grandfather was immediately swept up into his classified work and she found herself alone with Bryon, her baby son, my father, in a place where she had no friends and no family.

Her voice grows soft and wistful as she describes the snow falling hard and deep in that first mountainous winter, and the ice crystallizing on the inside walls of the Denver Steel housing unit that the government had assigned them—a prefabricated and barely insulated shack of corrugated metal. It was lonely. It was claustrophobic. She missed her father and her friends in California.

The government had told her she only needed a security clearance to begin her new life of opportunity and status, and each day she checked the mailbox for news of it. She had never wanted to be a housewife, had barely even wanted to be a mother, a fact she would later bring up often to punctuate feminist lectures in front of uncomfortable-looking family members. She had always seen herself as a woman with a career. But each day, she checked the mailbox, and each day passed with no answer.

I share 25 percent of my DNA with my grandmother, as we all do with all our grandmothers. Meaning that one-fourth of me is her. I look at my hands and wonder, Which parts? There is no physical resemblance, as far as I can tell, but maybe there are a multitude of subtle features: the shape of my ear, the length of my fingers, the weakness in my eyes. Or maybe my internal organs are a perfect match; maybe we have identical gallbladders and kidneys and I'll never know.

My guess is that the lion's share of her genetic traits have come bubbling up in my brain chemistry. The depression, the sudden clouding anger, yes, we both have that. Although she has become calmer in her old age, there are enough stories of her throwing plates of food across the kitchen or acidly tearing down my grandfather in front of family members and guests for me to know that the rage that infected my father and then me was in her too. In fact, I recently discovered that we are on the same type of antidepressants.

But this is drifting toward personality, which surely must be on the "nurture" side of the equation. Of course, her influence is strong in my upbringing. I spent most of my childhood summers at her house in the Santa Fe hills. To what degree does she influence me there? Twenty-five percent, again? At least. The reading, the love of the natural world, the oversensitivity to other's offhand comments, the social anxiety. Yes, she is here inside me.

And my son, Bryce, holds one-eighth of her somewhere in his tiny three-year-old body, nestled down, deep inside the one-half of him that is me, like a little bottle of someone I love enveloped inside of someone else I love.

I look at him, lean of body like my grandfather, full of an intense energy like my father. I hope that he has my grandmother's independent spirit, her unwillingness to accept the role that society carved out for her. I can't recall ever seeing her in a dress, and certainly she had no desire to be a passive participant in her marriage. She prickled against any condescension from her husband, held her own in any fight. She was clearly the dominant member of the household.

But then there was her anger. The clipped, venomous cursing, the sudden explosions of bilious rage when something didn't go her way or she felt she had been slighted. I remember her lecturing my grandfather for some misdeed, real or imagined; he sat at the table, tight-lipped, with a furrowed brow while she called him stupid, while she slammed her hands on the table and cursed.

He waited until she was done, and then silently left the room.

There was a reason that her mailbox had been empty each day: her application had been caught in the teeth of the AEC. "No individual shall be employed . . . until the Federal Bureau of Investigation shall have made an investigation and report . . . on the character, associations and loyalty of such an individual," stated the congressional act that created the AEC to rise from the wartime ashes of the Manhattan Project, and the commission took those words seriously.

There was cause for this. Even in the depths of World War II, when the very existence of Los Alamos and the goings-on there had been hidden from the knowledge of all but a few military and government officials, the Manhattan Project had been lousy with spies. Machinist David Greenglass delivered rough schematics of the bomb's implosion device to Soviet courier Harry Gold in an Albuquerque boarding house; physicist Theodore Hall, who at nineteen was the youngest scientist to be recruited into the project, slipped into the Russian embassy in New York shortly after being assigned to Los Alamos and announced his intention to funnel information to Moscow; and most damaging of all, Klaus Fuchs, a theoretical physicist with access to the most vital and classified work being done on the bomb, had met with Harry Gold and divulged everything he knew.

There is a famous photograph of Klaus Fuchs, a black-and-white snapshot used on his Los Alamos security badge. He gazes at the camera, slight of features, pale of skin, eyes bleary behind coke-bottle glasses, his head tilted unaccountably to the left. Is his expression defiant? Duplicitous? Tortured? I want to give him the benefit of the doubt and say "tortured." When British military intelligence interrogated him in January of 1950, the man broke down in tears and spilled it all with only the slightest urging from his interviewer. He was ashamed, he said. He had believed in the USSR and the ideals that it supposedly represented, but Stalin had ruined everything.

In late February of 1953, after months of waiting and as the bitter winter overstayed its welcome and yet another snowfall clogged the roads, Bernice made a phone call to Personnel Security to ask about the status of her application. A few days later, Willie Ortiz, a diminutive Hispanic man from the tiny nearby town of Chimayó and chief of the Los Alamos National Lab security branch, stopped by the house and told her that there was a problem.

She should soon expect a letter from the AEC. A week later, it came, alerting her to the fact that there were aspects of her past that concerned them. And then after a month, an agent of the AEC met with her personally.

Her memory of the first meetings with AEC representatives is hazy and confused, muddled together with later, more dramatic hearings. I know from oblique references in later letters from the AEC that she met with at least one representative on two occasions: first on April 9, and then on May 22, of 1953. Whether those meetings were held in Los Alamos or Albuquerque is not clear from the terse mention, but my guess is that it was a low-key, almost informal discussion at a Los Alamos location, perhaps even my grandparents' home. Certainly, by my grandmother's telling, she didn't think too much of it, despite the potentially serious consequences. She was calm as the representative asked her to clarify a few things from the list of past affiliations she had provided with her application to the lab. In particular, he was concerned about her membership in the Progressive Citizens of America while she attended classes at Los Angeles City College. He wanted to know about her tutelage under a sociology professor by the name of Herbert Alexander. And finally, he asked about her support for Progressive Party candidate Henry Wallace during the 1948 presidential election.

Once the meeting was over, she thought the matter was resolved, and that the delay over her clearance was a mere hiccup before the inception of her career. "After the first meetings, I thought it was settled," she tells me. After all, the questions the agent raised were about perfectly legal activities, protected by the Constitution.

At the table, she chuckles to herself, then adds, "When I received notice for the full hearing, then I knew that we were in deep shit."

Klaus Fuchs met Harry Gold on a bridge near the Santa Fe Plaza and handed him a briefcase full of secrets. I walked across that bridge many times with my grandmother when I was a child, looking over the rail at the thin trickle of the Santa Fe River.

Harry Gold met with machinist David Greenglass in the upstairs bedroom of a house near the University of New Mexico, where both my parents and I later attended school. He convinced Greenglass to sketch out the portion of the atomic bomb's implosion device that he was working on. I drove by the place a few days ago, stopping my car to look at the two-story bungalow on a hill overlooking Albuquerque's small downtown. The house is now called the Spy House. It's a bed-and-breakfast, and if you stay in Greenglass's old room, you can watch television on a set propped up on the desk where he drew the rough diagram of the bomb.

The world is littered with stories of the past, accumulating like fallen leaves.

When I called and asked my grandmother if she still had the letters and transcripts from her security hearings, she said that she hadn't been able to find them in years. I must have sounded disappointed, because she apparently started hunting for them in the various nooks and crannies of her Santa Fe house right after I hung up. A couple of hours later, she called me and announced that she had located them. "They were in a plastic bag under my bath mat!" she said, adding that she'd put them there so that they'd be safe.

A few days later, I had them in my hands. A manila envelope, my grandmother's handwriting scrawled across it in blue pen, "Info on *Hearings*, 1952–1955 (Security hearings)." Inside were several bundles of papers in plastic baggies and constrained with rubber bands: letters on thin typing paper (some stamped "OFFICIAL USE ONLY" above the words "United States Atomic Energy Commission"); a brown pamphlet entitled "In the Matter of J. Robert Oppenheimer"; a booklet of a few dozen thin sheets held together with rusting staples, its blue cover reading, "BEFORE THE PERSONNEL SECURITY BOARD."

It felt strange to finally be looking into this story. Despite the fact that it had been common knowledge in the family for years, I didn't really know anything about it apart from the broad outlines as described by my grandmother in offhand comments, usually when she was angry at some political situation or feeling persecuted. But here it was, something tangible that had its own objective existence apart from her stories, something that would allow me to fill in the holes in both my understanding and her remembered accounts. And more than that, to get a glimpse of her life long before I could have known her. An artifact, a connection, a conduit to the past.

As I opened the blue booklet and read through its thin, typewritten pages, I realized that it was that final reason—the desire to know who she was decades before my own life began—that was most important to me.

It's only a matter of time now before she is gone. Her mind is still fierce and quick, but her body is deteriorating. I don't know how long she has. Another leaf, poised to fall.

Because of that, these moments where I sit at the table and ask about her days waiting for word from the AEC, or when I thumb through the thin, half-century-old documents in the manila envelope, feel like a glimmering treasure that will soon disappear forever. I want to catch it, to hold it for a moment before it's gone.

I bundled the papers back into the envelope and placed them in my desk drawer, feeling as though I were securing an object of immeasurable value.

After the first meetings regarding her clearance, a full year passed before my grandmother heard back from the AEC. 1953 changed to 1954, and my grandparents began to settle into their new Los Alamos lives. They moved from the frigid Denver Steel house to a more solid and evenly heated duplex on Thirty-Sixth Street; my grandfather began important work on the triggering devices for hydrogen bombs; Bernice took a part-time job at the local library; her son turned three years old.

My father. He was three years old in 1954 in Los Alamos, thick bodied and brown haired, willful and intelligent. Twenty-five years later, in 1979, I would be three years old in Los Alamos. And now, as I sit at the table with my grandmother, I am thirty-five, and I can hear my own three-year-old son's voice from the other room as he describes the adventures of his toy trains to anyone in earshot.

My grandmother tells me that one of the reasons she wanted to stay in Los Alamos so badly, despite the loneliness, the uncertainty of her employment, and her growing discomfort with the horrors of nuclear weapons, was that she couldn't imagine a better life for her children than the one they had in New Mexico. As crime and congestion grew in Los Angeles through the 1950s and '60s, her children played in the mountain forests of an idyllic, government-run town.

As 1954 wore on and the family took trips into the alpine forests of the Jemez Mountains for picnics and hikes, they began to feel less isolated, less like outsiders in this strange community, and my grandmother's depression began to ease. When, in early 1954, she was offered a part-time job at the Los Alamos Medical Center assisting with autopsies, among other nonclassified duties, it seemed like it was only a matter of time before she received official word from the AEC that her clearance difficulties were a thing of the past.

But on April 15, a letter from the commission arrived, and it did not contain good news.

She stood beside her kitchen table in the small duplex, slicing open the envelope and pulling out the four sheets of the letter with shaking hands. "Dear Mr. and Mrs. Bannerman," it began, "In accordance with Section 10 of the Atomic Energy Act of 1946, an investigation has been conducted concerning the character, associations and loyalty of Bernice E. Bannerman. Certain information obtained as a result of this investigation has created a question concerning the eligibility of Bernice E. Bannerman for security clearance and employment on Atomic Energy Commission work and has also raised a question with respect to the continuance of Daniel E. Bannerman's security clearance and employment on Atomic Energy Commission work."

Following this threat are two pages listing activities that the FBI had uncovered that cast doubt on my grandmother's character: "Bernice E. Bannerman listed membership in the Progressive Citizens of America from 1947 to 1949"; "It was reported that she had been invited to attend a Communist Party meeting"; "It was reported that she had been on the mailing list of the Progressive Citizens of America"; "At one time, she received a publication such as 'USSR' or 'Soviet Russia Today.'" The final page contained two entries that especially stung her, as there seemed no doubt that they had come from interviews with friends and former neighbors: "It was reported that Bernice E. Bannerman stated to a person who was attending Los Angeles City College: 'I will fight on the right side—the side that will win if there is ever a war.' This statement was interpreted to mean that she would fight on the side of any foreign power with whom the United States might become engaged in war if she felt that the chances of that foreign power winning the war were better than those the United States." "It was reported . . . that Bernice E. Bannerman and Daniel E. Bannerman were closely associated with Lester and Selma Grossman . . . [who] had an unfavorable reputation in the vicinity of 16011 Leadwell Street, Van Nuys, California, and were considered to be 'Communists.'"

"You are both requested to make a written response to the above information," the letter concluded, "which should be submitted to me within ten (10) days of your receipt of this letter." It then closed in a manner incongruous with the subject matter, "Very Truly Yours, Donald J. Leehey."

They wasted little time sending letters of their own to the AEC requesting a formal hearing before the Personnel Security Board, as was their right under the commission's regulations. They also attempted to answer the charges in writing.

"I would like the opportunity to appear before a Personnel Security Board," stated my grandmother. "It would give me a chance to re-state my allegiance to the United States. In my own mind there *never* has been the slightest doubt as to my allegiance to this country!"

And yes, that's right. Although I've always known my grandmother as highly critical of the government, of capitalism, of the armed forces, I have never doubted that she is loyal to the ideals that this country was founded on. And yes, she is also a socialist, and has been her whole life. She is a firm believer in the social safety net, a proponent of universal health care, and her disappointment with President Obama stemmed from her view that he was not liberal enough.

Her views are such an integral part of her personality that I've never really considered that they must have an origin. At the dining room table, as my son—now outside—yells in the distance, I ask her, "Where did your attraction to socialist causes come from, exactly?"

She thinks for a moment, then in a soft voice she answers. "My father. My upbringing. He was a socialist . . . a union organizer. Very left of center. He was in demonstrations trying to organize the carpenters' union in Los Angeles in the 1930s, and law enforcement outnumbered them five to one and they were rough. I remember that he would come home with bruises on his arms and everywhere."

She pauses again. "But he wasn't a communist. We lived next door to a communist and he just yelled all the time, 'What this country needs is a communist government!' But my father said that was ridiculous."

"What did your father think of the USSR?" I ask.

"He thought they had a good idea behind them, but he drew the line at their oppression. They went too far."

The early years of the USSR must have seemed like a noble experiment to many people. A place where the ideals of shared labor and shared reward could be put to the test for all the world to see. And of course, the USSR was our great ally in World War II, the liberators of Berlin, the force that turned the tide. Roosevelt himself had said, during the war, "I believe . . . [Stalin] will work with me for a world of democracy and peace."

How disappointing it must have been when Stalin's true self became apparent.

I picture my grandparents in their Los Alamos bed, Bernice wide awake and worrying about her letter to the commission as my grandfather sleeps. She nudges him awake. He starts, props himself on his elbows, and asks "What the hell's wrong with you?"

"Dan, if this doesn't go through, you won't be able to work at a gas station in Lordsburg," she says in the darkness.

"It's just a threat; they would never do it," he answers and then lies back down. But she is not so sure that he believes it. In the other room, my father cries out in his sleep, then falls back to silence.

And then it was August of 1954 and my grandmother was twenty-seven years old and boarding a plane on the tuff mesa and it was not yet dawn and the mountain air was crisp and she was nervous and worried about leaving her three-year-old son behind with a sitter she barely knew and my grandfather was there and thirty-six years old, and maybe they held hands as they were escorted onto the small prop plane.

And soon they were flying and arcing south over the Jemez Mountains. As the sun rose, she watched through the airplane window. The pine forests dropped down and gave way to the arid and sandy Rio Grande Valley below.

A half hour after it had left Los Alamos, the plane landed on the dusty expanse of Albuquerque's east mesa. After taxiing for a few moments, the plane came to a stop near the airport terminal and stairs were wheeled out to meet it. My grandparents descended onto the tarmac and were escorted into a waiting AEC car. From the airport, the driver took them a short distance to the AEC's Operations Office at 4001 Gibson Boulevard SE, where the Personnel Security Board hearing was scheduled to commence at 8:15 a.m.

Inside the building, a husky guard took them to a meeting room where the Personnel Security Board assembled: Chairman A. L. Gausewitz, the dean of the University of New Mexico's School of Law; Lloyd Kersey of the AEC; and Thomas Donnelly, president of New Mexico Highlands University in Las Vegas. Also present were L. R. Duncan, another AEC representative, and E. E. Greeson, the court reporter for the United States District Court, who transcribed the proceedings as they occurred.

I have the result of Greeson's handiwork with me, that blue-bound booklet of some forty pages, somewhat ragged, the staples slipping at the lower edge. And because of it, I can see the meeting in my mind's eye and hear the voices of my grandparents and their questioners fifty-seven years ago.

In its pages, my grandparents constantly interrupt each other, in precisely the same way that they did in their more advanced age. They're obviously very nervous, and overexplain any number of details, including the reason that certain letters from friends testifying on their behalf are in new envelopes ("We tore the heck out of most of the [old] envelopes," states my grandfather), and why one of the testimonials may contain errors ("He is totally blind, so if you find a couple of mistakes . . . he likely didn't let his secretary look it over for him. I think there is a word left out and a letter missing in the last line"). At the board's prompting, my grandmother delivers her opinions on people in the same unfiltered style that had caused no end of family amusement and embarrassment over the years—when asked about a roommate, she says, "Not too smart. I mean, not to say anything derogatory about her, but she had one thought in mind and that was her next date"—and my grandfather responds far too often with blunt innuendo: "She seemed to me like she sort of wanted to make a pass at me, but was a little bit afraid of Bernice," he says, about the same roommate. "Of course, I was willing to make a pass if I could get it, but she was, as Bernice said, a harum-scarum kid."

And then there are insights into my grandmother's political views, admittedly delivered under duress. When the board asks her about her interest in "racial issues," her response is heartwarmingly simple: "When I went to City College there was a sorority . . . and I went to several functions there and came across some of this racial business, where these people were forbidden to enter the sorority because they were Negroes or Japanese. I couldn't see the reason in this and I still can't . . . I have never read a good argument yet that would substantiate any reason to segregate."

However, when the inquirer follows up by asking her, "Would you would want your daughter to marry a Negro?" her answer is an interesting capitulation: "I would recommend against it for one reason . . . our society is still along this line . . . it isn't accepted, and therefore I wouldn't want my daughter to be subjected to the prejudice and feeling that would go along with it."

The board's main interest seems to be in Dr. Herbert Alexander, the sociologist who had inspired my grandmother, and who was facing his own anti-communist hearings in California around the same time, as well as Les and Selma Grossman, the "communist" couple they had associated with in Van Nuys. My grandmother expresses appreciation for Dr. Alexander's lecturing style—"He was one of those people that if he was talking about a rainstorm, he could fascinate you"—and his interest in issues of racial equality, but confirms that she knew nothing of his involvement with any communist groups. Regarding the Grossmans, my grandmother has little to say, not having known them very well, but my grandfather happily launches into a monologue that takes up four pages of the transcript detailing his friendship with Lester—from their membership in the UCLA Jabberwock Club, where they would read "poetry or prose or some foolishness and drink tea out of little cups," to their time hiking through the Southern California mountains, to their separate service during World War II, to Lester's job as a mail carrier. Other than a brief mention that my grandfather considered himself "much more radical" than Lester, politics hardly intrudes on his story, and I imagine the board members shifting in their chairs wondering when the monologue would either come to an end or arrive at the point. He ends his speech with the dissolution of the friendship upon Lester's marriage to Selma. He didn't care for Selma, he says, because she was "dogmatic," and, well, fat.

"I don't like fat women," he concludes, simply, and with a little further questioning about the Grossman's political beliefs, the board seems satisfied with the exhaustive details that my grandfather provided.

The questions from the board members are surprisingly superficial; rarely do they ever go deeper than to ask whether or not a person from their past was a communist or press for more details on their associations with certain figures such as Lou Franklin, the president of Progressive Citizens of America. As I read over the transcript, the hearing does seem like a formality, but if so, then why the need for threats against my grandfather's security clearance, or to hold the inquiry at all?

Finally, after two to three hours, by my grandmother's reckoning, the board is ready to conclude the proceeding. The chairman asks her if she has anything to add before adjournment. She reiterates that her time with Progressive Citizens of America was a passing phase. The chairman then asks, "How do you feel about security regulations?" And here, Bernice answers with an obsequiousness that shamed her later in life when she thought back on it. "There definitely has to be something done," she says. "Because it has been proven in too many instances people, both communists and otherwise, have gotten into good positions. I certainly am not the person to suggest any better method of serving people. I think it is a fair method of doing it."

Later, the board asked her to sign a document stating, essentially, that her leftist beliefs were merely the product of a youthful woman's being led astray by suspect academics. She did, and it bothered her for the rest of her life. She felt that she had taken the easy way out, that what she should have done was stand up for the beliefs that she still held and challenge the legitimacy of the review board. Instead, she made a choice to protect her family, to ensure my grandfather's continued position in Los Alamos, to give her son a childhood in a sheltered mountain community far away from the crime and sprawl of her native Los Angeles. And she never felt quite right about it.

It is a tiny moment, a few sentences in the transcript, and a signature on the later document, but for her it was an act of cowardice, a capitulation in the face of authority, and the reason that she could never speak of that time again without regret and shame and victimhood in her voice.

And, with that, the witnesses were thanked for their time, and the hearing was adjourned. My grandparents were instructed to await word of the board's final recommendation, then escorted back to the airplane.

A few months after the hearing, she received notice that her security clearance had been granted and that my grandfather's was no longer in jeopardy, but the original position she had been offered was no longer available.

Sitting at her kitchen table, she tears up as she speaks about those last statements she had made to the board. "They said, 'You had better shine in this hearing,' and that was the ultimate threat. The only reason I changed my view and gave them what they wanted at the end was because of the threat against Dan. That was the only reason."

"Did you resent that?" I ask.

"Yes. Oh yes. Very, very much."

There is anticlimax here, a story that had been built up in my mind now rendered down to bare facts. After hearing of this story for so many years and letting it get confused in my own mind—"My grandma was put on trial by Joseph McCarthy!" I remember telling my high school history class—to finally learn what actually happened is strange, like visiting a childhood home after many years away or finally seeing a television appearance of your favorite author. "No, that's not how they look, that's not how they sound. Who is this imposter?" In the end, she did not get her security clearance denied and they were not forced to leave Los Alamos. She and Dan were not branded communists and blacklisted. They were able to remain in the city and raise their children as they had hoped.

But in that moment when she made her statement, and in the months afterward as they waited for the board's decision, they did not know that. Instead, Bernice was afraid. She was hurt. It didn't matter where her story fell in the context of the time—the AEC had found "reason" to suspect her loyalty to the United States and they had found it by digging through her personal beliefs, the ones she inherited from her father, and they found those by speaking to people she knew. Some must have been people she considered friends and neighbors. They had betrayed her.

And then, worst of all, in the end, she had capitulated. Like all of us when faced with similar circumstances in our mind's eye, she had always thought she would stand up for her beliefs. That she would be a hero. As she told me at her table, "Sometimes I wish I had just told them to go fuck themselves."

And what if she had done just that? What is the price of a moment of symbolic heroism? What if she had set her jaw and refused to sign the document, refused to compromise on her perfectly legal ideals, refused to turn her back on her lawful and patriotic past? Would the board have followed through with their threats? She was not an agent of a foreign government. She had no intention to jeopardize her own or her husband's or her children's future. What if she had looked across the table, straight into Donald Leehey's eyes, and said "Go fuck yourself"?

These are questions she asks herself even today. And the answer comes back to her: She thinks it likely that they would have revoked my grandfather's clearance and the two of them would have departed Los Alamos in shame, perhaps branded as "communists" for the rest of their lives. For evidence of that, she needed to look no further than the one document stored under her bath mat that didn't directly concern her case: the brown, coffee-stained booklet titled "In the Matter of J. Robert Oppenheimer."

Oppenheimer, tall and thin, dark haired and dark eyed, had been the unlikely bohemian who headed the Manhattan Project during World War II, who had handpicked the scientific luminaries who gathered in the secret Los Alamos of the early 1940s, who had overseen every detail of the atomic bomb's development, and who had stood in the afterglow of the first nuclear detonation at Trinity Site and muttered the immortal words from the Bhagavad Gita, "Now I am become Death, the destroyer of worlds." He was, in other words, a living legend, a myth who had performed a herculean labor for his country by giving it the most devastating weapon the world had ever seen.

But after the war had reached its end, Oppenheimer had second thoughts about the power he had helped unleash. He began, privately, to speak against the bomb, telling President Truman, "I have blood on my hands." He lobbied for an international agency to control nuclear stockpiles so that no single country would be able to use it without oversight, including the United States. Most damningly, in the eyes of military hawks, he counseled against the development of a hydrogen fusion bomb, a weapon of far more destructive potential than the fission bomb created during the Manhattan Project.

And for that, he was pilloried, subject to his own Personnel Security Board hearings mere days before my grandmother received word of hers. His past was dug through, the organizations he had belonged to in California compiled into documents that served as the ammunition of a firing squad. Although there was never any proof that he had engaged in treasonous activities, Oppenheimer's enemies were determined to make an example of him. In 1954, the same year my grandmother faced her own security hearing, he was publicly humiliated and stripped of his clearance, sending a chilling message to government scientists in the age of McCarthy: None of you are safe.

The AEC published the pamphlet summarizing and clarifying its findings against Oppenheimer shortly after it handed down the verdict, which was met with widespread outrage in the scientific community. As Bernice awaited the scheduling of her hearing, it must have seemed especially pertinent to her, and when the board offered her an out through the simple admission of her youthful naïveté, it hurt her pride but must have also been a relief. The outcry against Oppenheimer's incrimination was strong and sudden. Editorialists throughout the country leaped to his defense, and portrayed the AEC as the bad guy. I can't help but wonder if things might have gone differently for her if the board had considered her case before Oppenheimer's concluded. Could it be that the agency suddenly realized that it overstepped its bounds? That it was now unwilling to doggedly pursue someone whose crimes appeared only to have been a controversial set of views?

I don't know the answer to that question, but I wonder if perhaps the Personnel Security Board shared my grandmother's sense of relief when she signed the final document and the matter was settled.

And there it was, a small moment that defined my family, one of an infinite number. A sacrifice Bernice made for her husband, for her children and grandchildren. Not huge, perhaps, but painful and important to her. And I can see it, can hear their voices as they went through that time of anxiety, another ripple spreading outward from a larger event.

It is now early afternoon as we sit at the table in Santa Fe, the New Mexico sun beaming through the windows some sixty years after all this happened. She's eighty-six years old, and worn out with talking—for the last half hour or so, she has been stammering her answers and trailing off, and I can tell it's time to stop. She has magazines to read, animals to feed, plants to water—her normal routine that takes up the days now.

I thank her for telling me these stories.

"I hope you got something you can use," she says, and walks to her chair in the sunroom.

4

Mythologies

When I was ten years old, I had a sanctuary. It was in my uncle Bruce's room at my grandmother's house in Santa Fe. There I would spend long hours with Bruce as he told stories from his vast store of knowledge. He was a gifted tale-teller and reveled in the obscure and beautiful, the motions of his hands accenting the pictures formed by his words. He had a deep love for exactly the things that could hold my attention at that age. When I read the *Lord of the Rings* for the first time, he talked to me about Tolkien's writings like they were a sacred text, delving into the myths and legends behind the story's creation as though he were speaking of the works of a prophet. Later, when I became interested in the diminutive world of insects, he rifled through his densely packed bookshelves and pulled out works like *Near Horizons* by American naturalist Edwin Way Teale and *The Book of Insects* by French entomologist Jean-Henri Fabre, and described their early experiments with ants and caterpillars in so much detail that it almost seemed like he had performed them himself. Sometimes, the conversational river we coursed down would swirl into unexpected eddies, as his desire for mysticism and meaning took us into the world of Vajrayana Buddhism, or my then-teenage interests drifted us to the Beat poets and the mystic philosophies of Carl

Jung and Joseph Campbell. As the night grew late, we cascaded through bodhisattvas and levitating monks, the heroic archetype and the wonders of an enlightened mind. I would come out of his room feeling unsteady as I tried to acclimate to the banal reality I lived in.

He collected books, obsessively so. His room was a floor-to-ceiling library with every available surface given over to piles of volumes. The cramped room was a miniature labyrinth, filled with mysterious crannies, innumerable significant objects—obsidian arrowheads, clay ocarinas, quartz beads, and *vajra* scepters beneath thick layers of dust. It was a forest of words and knowledge, a reflection of himself, bursting with untapped wisdom, a treasure trove of story.

He was also my guide through the wilds of New Mexico, especially the Jemez Mountains. He often took me hiking through secret places in the range, leaving the established trails for destinations that only he knew of and had named: "the Faerie's Aisle," "the Mirthful Brook," "Small Mountain." Along the way, he would ruminate about the patterns of nature, the eyes of aspen trees watching us from the green world all around, and his fears of how the modern world would disrupt a natural harmony.

In the center of the Jemez Mountains there is an enormous meadow, a land of grass and gentle breezes that stretches for thirteen miles across, enclosing streams, small copses of aspen, and grazing elk in a green wreath around a domed peak. It seems like one of the most beautiful, peaceful places in the world. But this peacefulness is an illusion, an accident of time and geology.

The meadow's name is the Valles Caldera. It is a volcanic crater.

Let me take a moment now and let Bruce explain. Because if anybody knows this valley, it is him.

Here we are: I am twelve and Bruce and I are driving to the Jemez, for a hike, for a meander, for a slow walk in the woods. But just after we cross the red and sluggish Rio Grande and begin our ascent along the side of the bare canyon that leads up to the high mountains, Bruce interrupts himself in the middle of whatever he was saying and blurts out, "We have to stop here!"

He turns sharply off the road and onto a dusty shoulder. "Come on," he says, unbuckling himself and leaving the car. Surprised by the sudden stop, I take a moment longer to remove my own belt. Outside, Bruce has already stalked off of the shoulder toward some cliffs on the canyon wall and is running his delicate hands over the chalky white rock. Wondering what is happening, I exit the car and join him.

"OK, so this is ash, right? Tuff. I was just reading about this," he begins. "It's amazing."

"From the volcano?" I ask.

"Yes!" He turns to me and gives his slightly crooked-toothed smile. "It's amazing. One and a half million years ago, on a windless day—-and that's the best part of the whole story, right there, that they know it was a windless day a million and a half years ago," and he laughs in his nervous way, and puts his hands together and makes a sort of egg shape with the space between them. "The way a huge volcano like the one that formed the Jemez works is that it builds up pressure in a big chamber underneath." Here he pushes his hands forward and I see that the empty space between them was meant to be the chamber. "And it builds up more and more and the chamber is closed up, so the pressure can't go anywhere, it just builds and builds and builds. So you know how a soda bottle, when it's just sitting on a shelf, it doesn't have any bubbles in it? But when you open it, the bubbles come out of solution, and you can either open it slowly and it just sort of fizzes out, or, if you shake it up real hard and then open it, it will all come bursting out, exploding, and you can wind up with an empty bottle and soda all over the room? The great magma chamber under the mountain was pressurized like that soda bottle, and on that *windless day*, one million years ago, there was a little earthquake or something that sent a crack down into the chamber, and that pressurized vault started to release all at once and the magma came bursting into the air."

Then he turns back to the mountain range ahead of us, raises his hand and sweeps it up into the sky, and for a moment he looks like a reed-thin symphony conductor in scruffy green jeans and an unbuttoned overshirt fluttering in the breeze. Watching his hands tracing an upward path against the blue, I can almost see the ash and smoke from that first eruption billowing up at least twenty thousand feet, straight in the air, before falling back down and settling evenly over the landscape ("And that's how they can tell that the day was windless, from how evenly it spread," he said). "And that first eruption, just a little one really, sent a crack farther down until it reached the huge chamber beneath everything, and, like the shaken soda bottle, all of the pressurized magma burst out in a second eruption, a gigantic one that sent a smoking fourteen-mile-wide column of steam and smoke and ash pouring outward. And it billowed and clouded and rained back down upon the earth and lava flowed over the ground until six hundred cubic *miles* worth of material settled on the surface." And here Bruce points to the layers of the canyon around us, and there that material is, striated vertically through the earth. "And the falling ash built the land up all around the now-empty magma chamber, a crater, huge and deep with sheer, straight sides, thousands and thousands of feet deep, and pieces of its remaining roof began crumbling down into the void, chunks of granite a full mile thick, four miles wide, crashing down into the cavern and striking the floor with a sonic boom that cracked stone for miles around.

"All that was left was an enormous, smoking pit surrounded by seventy miles of death and lava in every direction. A barren land, broken by the explosion.

"Slowly, it cooled down," Bruce continues. "The ash started to weld together, becoming the white tuff of these cliffs, right here! And the rain came and cut rivulets through the layers, digging grooves and ditches that became arroyos and then canyons like the one we are in right now. And the ground settled around the crater, and the rivers carried soil into the abyss and slowly filled it with sediment over thousands and thousands of years. And grass began to grow. And one day, the gaping maw of broken earth had amazingly become a green, fertile valley in the center of a craggy, pine-covered mountain range, a beautiful and peaceful place."

Bruce seems to collapse into himself, the animating power of the story leaves him, and his hands fall limply. The moment is gone. "Um, OK. Let's keep going," he says, hunching over and shoving his hands into his pockets before walking back to the car.

The town of Los Alamos sits atop a mesa formed from the petrified ash spewed by the Valles Caldera. Its location was originally chosen as much for its beauty as for its remoteness, nestled among ponderosa pine forests and stunning cliffs and canyons. Since its founding, it has grown into an idyllic, affluent, white-collar community in the heart of one of the poorest states in the nation, a small city that looms disproportionately large in our world.

It is also a place of great significance to my family. If dinner conversations, half-heard arguments, and idealized stories form a mythic cycle, then Los Alamos is our origin spot, the lost world we came from. When I visit, as I do every few years, I find that an air of unreality pervades it, and my memories of childhood there feel like a gauzy dream. In 1976, my parents moved into my grandparents' old house there, the very one where Bruce and my father were raised. We lived there for only a few years, but later, long after moving, when I suffered the typical stresses of middle and high school, as my parents' marriage began to suffer, and as my father's mental illness began to assert itself, I longed to go back to the strange city in the New Mexico mountains. Everything, I thought, had been right there. Beautiful. Peaceful.

But we never did return. Instead, my father worked unfulfilling jobs in Houston, Texas, before he died of a heart attack at the age of forty-three, and, eventually, my family came to Albuquerque, New Mexico, just on the other side of the Jemez, but far more than a world away.

I will never live there again; the ponderosa forests will never again be my forests in the way they were when I was a child. But I make a pilgrimage back from time to time.

Today is one of those pilgrimages. I am in middle age and riding with Bruce, again, in my grandmother's car as he curses at the steering wheel and drives up through the canyon to the plateau on which Los Alamos perches. We have already passed the tuff cliffs he showed me when I was twelve, but his thoughts are occupied by different concerns today.

"It's like, for so long I thought it was my place," he's saying. For Bruce, this feeling of exile is even more deeply rooted than it is for me. He spent his entire life until the age of eighteen in the city. "I thought that it belonged to me, but it's not like you can work there. Or live there. Unless you're in the lab," he says as the bottom of the canyon drops away on our right and the road climbs. "I always hated them for that."

"Hated who?" I ask.

"The fuckers who run the place," he says.

The road we are on now is an ancient one, originally used by the Native American people from the nearby Pueblos for hunting expeditions and religious pilgrimages. Later, Hispanic ranchers followed it to settle in the high mountains and graze livestock at the Valles Caldera. Then came privileged white teenage boys on horseback, sent from the East to live a simulacrum of pioneer life for a summer or so at the Los Alamos Ranch School. William S. Burroughs, Gore Vidal, and, fatefully, J. Robert Oppenheimer all traveled here in the first half of the twentieth century. And then, the mark of these mountains forever upon his soul, Oppenheimer, then a theoretical physicist, led a group of the United States' greatest scientists up the dusty, winding path that he remembered so fondly from his camp days and began a wartime mission to build a secret city dedicated to the creation of an atomic weapon.

The road curves its way up along the cliffs, and as we round a corner, it soars ever higher above the green canyon floor.

"Now this feels like home," Bruce says as the view unfolds before us. And he is right—even for me, who only lived in the Jemez Mountains for a few years of my childhood, it seems good and correct for those tuff cliffs of ancient, welded ash to be on our left and the sheer drop to the canyon bottom on the right.

"That patch down there, the mound? That's a Pueblo ruin," he says, slowing the car and pointing to an area in the canyon where the grass is a strikingly different shade of green.

"And that," he says, moving his finger to the right where a fenced-off area is just discernible below, "they've roped that off due to lanthanum contamination. Fred showed that to me."

I perk up at the mention of Fred, a friend of my grandparents' who often stayed with them. He was Native American, the governor of a nearby Pueblo who had formed a friendship with my family. "What ever happened to Fred, anyway?" I ask.

"Oh," Bruce answers, thoughtfully. "He died a few years ago, down in Mexico. Grandma took it pretty hard." (He always calls her "Grandma" or "Bernice" when he is speaking to me. Never "Mom.")

As I look down to the canyon's grassy floor, I think about Fred, with his leathery skin and easy smile. He had moved to Mexico in the seventies, but he'd almost always been at my grandparents' house when I visited them during the summers as a child. For some reason, he preferred to stay with them even as he visited a multitude of relatives in various New Mexico pueblos.

As we come out of the canyon and reach the top of the Pajarito Plateau, we pass the tiny Los Alamos Airport on the right, built atop a deposit of plutonium waste. To the left, a brown, square tower high above the tree line marks the Los Alamos Neutron Science Center, where subatomic particles are accelerated to 84 percent of the speed of light. I look at it, a feeling of amazement flitting across my mind, but I am also dwarfed, slightly ashamed by the fact that I don't exactly know why it is amazing. What does it do to a neutron to send it whizzing down a straight line at such an astounding speed? And the scientists who make it happen, what do they want, what do they hope it will do? The knowledge feels distant from me, and even though

I know I could go home and do some research and probably find out the basic theories and results of some of the experiments, I also realize that I will never really know it intimately like the scientists in the Neutron Science Center itself. Their knowledge, and their world, is locked away from me by its specialized nature, and, often, by its classified status, like so much of the city that we are now entering.

I wonder if Bruce feels the same way.

His degree was in biology, but he hasn't worked in a science-related field in decades, and the mystery cult of the lab is just as closed off for him.

And my father too. I know he felt shut out from this world, and I know it frustrated him. After years of working what amounted to odd jobs in Houston, he finally got his bachelor's degree in physics at the age of thirty-five. He immediately applied to the lab in Los Alamos, trying to come back to his hometown after ten years of exile in Texas. He was offered jobs, too, at the lab and at the defense contractor EG&G, but they were not high status or important enough for him. They were technician positions. He turned them down, unwilling to return to Los Alamos as anything less than a full-fledged scientist.

It had been different for their father. In 1952, Dan Bannerman, my grandfather, had been recruited from Los Angeles, and even though he had also only had a bachelor's degree, the recruiters had wanted him for his machinist skills, had sent him out to the town on their dime, and had made him promises, including assuring him full scientist status. But that was just less than a decade after World War II, when Los Alamos was a closed city and New Mexico seemed much more remote than it does now, necessitating such incentives. It was a world that disappeared soon after.

As Bruce drives toward the residential areas, I wonder if my father would have been happy even if we had come back here. Certainly, that unrealized hope seemed to gnaw at him. He was depressed and sometimes medicated and more often self-medicated. As the years went by, he started to avoid the family, sequestering himself in his tiny, cramped office when he was at home and other times just being absent until late at night, doing who knows what.

Before we come to the neighborhoods, Bruce makes another of his announcements. "Let's go down DP Road," he says, turning suddenly to the right.

The road, a short spur to a canyon rim, is named for the Delta Prime Site, where scientists conducted experiments around the refinement of plutonium from 1945 to 1978. In 1958, a man named Cecil Kelley had died there in a terrible accident. He had been standing on a footstool, monitoring a solution of plutonium and various organic solvents and acids in a stainless-steel tank, when there was a sudden blue flash. Two other technicians ran into the room to find that Kelley had been knocked off his ladder and now lay on the floor, muttering, "I'm burning, I'm burning" over and over again. Somehow, the plutonium had gone critical, and Kelley absorbed a fatal dose of alpha radiation. He died thirty-five hours later, and the medical office removed his organs and sent them to other laboratories for analysis before they were buried inside a number of lead-lined drums. By the 1970s, the buildings themselves were declared to be too contaminated for further use, and like Kelley's body, they were dismantled, disseminated, analyzed, and disposed of.

"Your dad used to like to come down here," Bruce says as we drive down the road, a narrow, unassuming street lined with car repair shops, industrial-looking warehouses, and empty lots that extend to the rim of the nearby canyon. "There were a bunch of mechanics and he and his friends would come down and chat with them about cars or whatever. Fred had a trailer here for a while when his wife kicked him out too."

As we drive, a wide field, scraped down to bare earth behind a chain link fence covered in warning signs, catches my eye. It is a part of the old DP Site itself, where the clean-up crew has attempted to remove all contaminated earth. Beyond the fence, a huge warehouse with ventilation pipes and ducts sticking out from its roof looms over the scene. Bruce stops, and we step out of the car and set off at his characteristic lope.

As we come closer, I see that the warehouse is fitted with a set of wheels, each one taller than a person. Because, as we see through the chain link, this massive warehouse itself is mobile, fitted with pneumatic lifts so that it can be raised and placed over a contaminated area to contain the radioactive dust kicked up from the cleanup. The large filtration vents along the side let air in, but keep dust from leaving. And behind this warehouse are five just like it.

"Should we be here? Is it safe?" I ask.

"Well, you know," Bruce answers. "It's Los Alamos; that shit is everywhere."

Not exactly comforted, I walk with Bruce back to the car. The shit is everywhere. That's clear enough.

Finally, we come to the neighborhoods and drive down winding streets through housing developments that look like old pictures of Levittown: boxy, two-story homes with flat faces and asbestos siding.

Bruce slows again. "Don Usner's house was right here, between us and the fence," he says, referring to a friend he still keeps in touch with, whom I also know. "His father died a few years back before the fire, you know."

He's talking about the Cerro Grande Fire, a massive, wild inferno that destroyed hundreds of homes in Los Alamos and thousands of acres of forest.

"But before he passed," Bruce continues, "he called Don to come to his house, saying that there were things Don needed to know about before he died. Don arrived and his dad took him down to the locked basement and showed him cans filled with black powder and .50-caliber machine gun shells and even a few live, loaded artillery shells, things he had collected over his years in the lab. 'If there's a fire,' he said to Don. 'You need to come in here and get this stuff out.'" Bruce laughs, then continues, "Two years later, his dad was gone, and the fire came and his mom was still there and she ran in and got the paperwork, the history of her family in Chimayó, but left everything else, including all these beautiful bonsai trees Mr. Usner made, beautiful bonsai aspens he had grown that were three inches high and would turn yellow in the fall, and they left it all. And the firemen came to suppress the flames that came roaring down into the neighborhood, but Usner's house began to pop and flare outward so the firemen backed away as far as they could, and just watched as it exploded."

Not far past the Usners' lot is our old family house on Thirty-Fifth Street, where both Bruce and I lived at different times—the closest thing we have to an ancient family home. It's plain for an ancient estate, a 1950s government-made two-story rectangle with large central picture windows on both top and bottom floors. We get out of the car and stand on the shoulder of the road right in front of the steep ditch that runs beside it.

Bruce takes out his camera, an expensive Canon, drops to one knee, and begins taking pictures of the house. As he does, he tells me how the yard looked when he was a kid, how he and my father would play in the pine trees behind it and dig foxholes in the sandy ground.

"Shall we take a walk around back?" Bruce asks as he finishes the round of photos.

"Can we do that? It's OK?"

"Of course," he answers, not even giving it a moment of thought, as though the fact that other people live here now simply doesn't factor into the decision.

We clamber down the little gully, once filled with pine trees that were all burned in the Cerro Grande Fire, and then back up the other side and into the wild area behind the lot. Back there, some of the pines still stand, though their bark bears scorch marks. Bruce stalks through the undergrowth, heading straight for the backyard of the old house.

"Here!" he announces, pointing up at one of the larger pines. "See that groove in the branch? That's from a tire swing Bryon made in the fifties."

The mental image of that tire swing hanging from a stately ponderosa brings the feeling of mountain idyll rushing back to me. "I wish we had lived here longer," I say. "I always felt that I had been cheated out of something."

"That's interesting," Bruce says. "Because when Bryon got that job transfer to Houston, I couldn't believe it. I told him, 'You're going the wrong direction! The only direction to go is either west or north, and especially west.'" It's a little strange to hear Bruce talk about my father. There's an edge of anger to his voice, and frustration.

My father was seven years old and deeply resentful of Bruce when he was born. The family lore is filled with examples of my father's cruelty toward his younger brother. For instance, one of my father's cousins told me about a time that he and Bryon had trapped seven-year-old Bruce in a pit they were digging for a basement and how Bruce had cried and cried as they rained dirt down on him from above. "I stopped and asked Bryon why we were doing it and he just kept shoveling the dirt down on Bruce, grinning like a crazy person. And Bryon was fifteen!" But through the cruelty, he somehow also became a paternal figure for Bruce. Bryon's death at the age of forty-three hit Bruce hard, and only sharpened the point of anger he felt toward his older brother. I vividly remember him speaking at my father's memorial, laughing and crying as he struggled to speak comprehensibly, wiping the snot off his nose with the sleeve of his shirt.

"I always thought he'd have been happier if he'd gone to California. But it was like, nah, he didn't want that," Bruce continues. "He didn't want to pursue a path that might increase creativity or consciousness."

If only he'd gone to California. If only he'd gotten a job at the lab. If only we hadn't left Los Alamos. If only he had gone to the doctor more often and addressed his heart disease. If only he hadn't drank so much. Any discussion of my father is laced with these hypotheticals.

Bruce walks on without explaining any further. He's still angry, I can tell. Angry at my father for having left. Maybe angry at himself for having actually gone to California for a few years, then returning to my grandparents' house.

I catch up to him, despite his quick stride. "Did you guys ever get along?" I ask.

Bruce stops walking for a moment and peers up into the pine needles. "Sure," he said. "When we started smoking pot."

"When was that?"

"I guess I must have been thirteen and he was twenty. He and your mom gave it to me."

"Really?" I ask in disbelief. "Isn't that a little young?"

Bruce chuckles then. "No, it was great. It was like we were finally together on something. Like we could share in the experience and hide it from the world. I loved it. Of course, I probably smoked way too much in my life. But in those days, it was great. And it helped him too, you know. He was so much calmer when he was high. All that anger would disappear and he would be fun to be around."

We are both quiet for a long moment. If only my father had smoked more pot. For some reason, I suddenly think of something that first came to mind when we were back at the canyon. "Hey, Fred lived with you guys for a while, didn't he?"

"Um, yeah," Bruce answers. "Let's see. When I was an infant. Fred was there to change my diaper, that sort of thing. I remember that."

"How long?" I say.

"Hmmm. I don't remember, really. It's one of those things that Bryon knew." He is quiet again, then adds, "I actually talked to him about it maybe one time, about . . . we were hanging around the Houston International Airport waiting for somebody, and we actually had a fairly frank conversation about what life was like when I couldn't remember."

Bruce stops again. Then nods his head twice, as if agreeing to something inside his own mind, deciding to go ahead and say something that he's been thinking over. "Bryon said that . . . that Fred and Bernice . . . Grandma . . . did have a thing. An affair."

"Really?" I ask, surprised.

"Yeah." He looks embarrassed to be telling me, but he continues. "It was very painful for everybody. But Fred and Dan, they managed to be close friends after that whole time. Everybody tolerated an intolerable thing."

"That's kind of amazing, isn't it? That everybody wound up OK?"

"It got bad, though. Loud and bad. Even years later. They were such stormy people. Fred was stormy, Bernice was stormy, Dan had to be stormy just to keep up. Many loud 'discussions.' And your father and Fred's son, Freddie Jr., they would fight all the time. Because everybody knew that

Bernice was having an affair with Fred, and Freddie knew it gave him power. And it made Bryon so goddamned mad."

We've walked through the woods a little ways now, down an old path toward a golf course behind the house.

I feel quiet, not knowing what else to say. "So much yelling. I remember that," Bruce says, almost abruptly. "I remember Bernice asking me, when I was little, maybe three years old, to go and tell Fred not to leave. He was in the other room getting ready to move out, and she was crying and she asked me to tell him not to leave. And she wanted ME to do it. I was three years old."

We are both quiet again. I don't know what to say at all. My mother once referenced the affair, obliquely, but I didn't know if it was true or if I had just misunderstood her. "Grandma gave Dan an ultimatum," she had said. "Either Fred got to move in or she would move out."

Then we both fall quiet again. The wind blows through the remaining pine needles. Our footsteps push through the underbrush.

"My mother used to take me walking back here when I was about three," I say. "It seemed like such an epic trail when I was little, when all the trees were still here. One of my earliest memories was carrying a toy plane through the woods here on an autumn day. Everything just seemed so peaceful."

"I spent many days playing around here too," Bruce answers. "There's a wet area just past this where there were hundreds and hundreds of garter snakes."

As we walk out onto the green of the golf course, he adds, "Of course, it turned out later that the water was mildly radioactive."

Bruce has one last stop in mind before we head out of town. Just around the corner from the old neighborhood, there's a surplus shop called the Black Hole. As we pull into the driveway, I can't help but laugh at the amazing collection of arcane junk that litters the lot, to the extent that it takes me a moment to even see the store itself behind it all. Old computers; gigantic laboratory cameras; chunks of hospital equipment with radiation symbols still fixed to their outsides; a wheelbarrow full of bowling balls; a strange and huge barrel-like container that's at least ten feet in diameter and lying on its side, waiting to roll over the whole operation; a Civil Defense–issued drum that once contained sealed and sterile water for a fallout shelter ("TO REUSE AS A COMMODE" reads the last paragraph of instructions on its army-green surface); and a handful of old bomb and missile casings, some of which have been repurposed into a sculpture of a giant sunflower.

"A guy named Ed Grothus started this place," Bruce says as we wander around the grounds. "He also used to run the Shalako Shop that your parents used to buy jewelry at. Look"—Bruce points to a large A-frame building on the other side of a pile of discarded electronics—"that used to be a church of some kind, but let's go see it now."

We climb up a short hill and stand before the building. It's clearly an old church, but just as clearly, it is in terrible disrepair. Two bomb casings, split in half as though broken over a giant's knee, are mounted on metal poles to either side of the church's entrance, and a large blue sign stands before the door.

> OMEGA PEACE INSTITUTE
>
> FIRST CHURCH OF HIGH TECHNOLOGY BLACK HOLE SYNOD
>
> Critical Mass Every Sunday
>
> with
>
> Bomb Unworship Service

We walk to the front of the building, but it is clear that there is no worship, or "unworship," happening here. A fist-sized hole has been broken into the frame around the door, and written in marker is a warning, or perhaps a plea: "There is nothing in this building that will bring quick easy cash! I know! —Ed Grothus"

"He must have died five years ago," Bruce says. "He came out here to build bombs but had a change of heart and became a peace activist. Somewhere around here he used to have these enormous obelisks that he had carved with some kind of peace message. I wonder if they're still here?"

We walk back down the hill and enter the store. Grothus's son is working the floor, trying to hustle people out for closing time. When he comes to us, I ask him how much he wants for the Civil Defense water drum.

"Not for sale," he answers, then, "Listen, I'm trying to get out of Dodge here."

"Sure," Bruce, says, but still asks, "Say, are those big obelisks still here?"

The son shakes his head and looks annoyed for a moment. Then he says, "I've got them around back, but I ain't opening them up."

He starts to turn away from us, then swivels back. He shakes his head. "I'll tell you though, if YOU are ever going to get two three-ton obelisks with peace messages written on them in twenty-six different languages, just make sure that you ALSO have an idea of where you're going to put them before you die."

"Where did he want to put them?" I ask.

"I don't know. I think he just figured you could stick them anywhere, but no, the county ain't going to let that happen. So I'm stuck with them. What the hell am I supposed to do with 'em? The cart was so far in front of the horse the horse couldn't even see it." And then he was gone, ushering others out of the building.

On the way back out, Bruce again falls into silence. I understand why. Los Alamos is our lost hometown, but no longer a place for us. The old cliché is that one can never go home again, but that's not entirely true. In most cases, what it means is that, although you can return to the places of your upbringing, they will have irrevocably changed and you can never recapture what they meant for you. But Los Alamos is different. It's a city built for a select set of purposes: to test scientific theories related to the design and manufacture of America's nuclear stockpile. Other people live there besides scientists, of course, but they are still there to support that industry. We, the children and grandchildren of the bomb, are locked out as surely as we are locked out from the steel gates that secure the technical areas.

Before we descend from the mesa, Bruce again stops at the pullout over the lanthanum-contaminated canyon. We silently step out of the car and look down on the grass and pines below us. The air is still, the trees motionless. Bruce remains quiet.

After a few moments, I ask him, "What did you think? Of going back?"

"Hmmm . . ." he answers. "It's tough, you know. There's a lot of stuff there. For so long I wanted to come back, but I don't know . . . it's not really for me anymore."

I nod.

"And you know, there's just so much stuff there. Seeing the old house . . . I don't know, I just wonder who I would have been if we'd lived anywhere else." He continues, "We get stuck with so much baggage from our childhoods. I mean, nothing too terrible ever happened, so many people have it worse. But still, what are we supposed to do with it all? And I hated that you guys left." He shakes his head.

I think about the eruption and the ash falling down, how the world here had changed because of it. The smoking hole and the piling tuff. The rain cutting through it all, making canyons, cliffs, filling the abyss with silt until today it's a meadow, green and soft. But underneath it all, the magma remains, a growing pool in a chamber of mounting pressure.

5

Nuclear Pilgrimage

In the predawn dark of July 16, 1945, the barren plain of the Tularosa Basin in central New Mexico was lit by a sudden explosion of light. A burning cloud spread outward from the top of a metal tower that was quickly incinerated in the intense heat. The explosion roiled up into the sky, touched by green, red, and orange, brighter than the sun itself.

Seventy years later, there is hardly anything to see at the site of that hellish detonation, not even a crater. Yet the Trinity Site has become a strange tourist attraction. On the one or two days a year it is open to the public, thousands of visitors line up in RVs, family sedans, SUVs and motorcycles to enter a restricted military base, drive a half hour through the desert, and finally stand in the center of a flat, mostly empty circle of ground surrounded by fences and signs warning of harmful levels of radiation.

On April 4 of this year, a windy spring Saturday, my fellow weekly newspaper employee Mark Lopez and I make the two-hour drive down to the turnoff to the site and then wait in an endless line of vehicles for over an hour to enter White Sands Missile Range's Stallion Gate. After an interminable crawl to the gate itself, soldiers perfunctorily check our identification and wave us through as protesters with signs memorializing family members who died of cancer stand silently nearby.

After another half hour of driving through the range, keeping our eyes open for the antelope that live there, wondering aloud about the purpose of the abandoned bunkers and other military structures we see scattered about, we come to the parking lot for the site. Hundreds of people mill about, taking pictures of the radiation signs along the outside of the fence that mark ground zero of the explosion, and examining the remnants of Jumbo, a gigantic metal cylinder that had been built to hold the Trinity device, but was never used. It reminds me of a music festival without music, as families talk and laugh and bikers pull in on their roaring hogs.

Inside the fence's perimeter, at ground zero, however, the crowd spreads out over the area, moving between the few "attractions" at the site: an obelisk of volcanic rock memorializing the detonation, a few scraps of melted metal that remained from the original tower, a replica of the Fat Man bomb dropped on Nagasaki, and a series of historic photographs posted along the fence. Some people bend over and hunt through the dust for pieces of Trinitite, shiny green rocks created when heat from the explosion fused the sand into glass. Beyond that, there's nothing really to look at.

I approach two women, one middle-aged, the other elderly. They tell me their names are Leticia and Josie Duran and they drove up from Las Cruces. I ask them about what they think of the site. "Just the history, just to see it," Leticia said. "It's . . . impressive."

"What do you think of the fact that we used a nuclear weapon on the Japanese?" I ask her.

"Before I came here, I thought, well, it was for our safety," she says, then thinks for a moment. "But then you see the protesters and it makes you think of the negative aspects of it. So I have mixed feelings."

I ask Josie, her mother, if she was alive during World War II and what she thought of the bomb at the time.

"It was exciting! We were all so happy," she answers eagerly. But she tells me that her thoughts have changed with time. "When you are young, it's different. But then you start to think about it as you get older, and it becomes kind of scary."

I continue to talk to people. Some have come from Mississippi, Georgia, all over the United States, and other parts of New Mexico. Others have come from overseas. I talk to bikers and families and members of the military.

The word "underwhelming" comes up again and again. And it is true; the site itself is underwhelming. A flat spot of ground on an endless flat plain. There are mountains rising up on the horizon, but they are miles away. Here, at the site itself, there is hardly anything but people searching for a way to connect to a moment that occurred seventy years ago.

The second thing that comes up with everyone I speak to is a somber undecidedness about the use of the bomb itself. No one I ask is utterly in favor of the Japanese bombings, nor is anyone completely opposed. Instead, they offer nuanced and uncertain views.

We stay for perhaps an hour, then make our way back to the dusty parking lot. As we drive away, the road is quieter now. The entry gate is closed for the day; the protesters have gone home. A short line of cars follows us out, including a police SUV.

Both Mark and I are silent as we make our way back to the road. "It's heavy," Mark finally says. "It's hard to believe that we used a nuclear bomb. I don't know what to think of it." We discuss the pros and cons of the bombings, and like those I spoke to at the site, it's hard for us to wrap our minds around it, and impossible to come down fully on one side or the other.

Suddenly, the cop car behind us turns on its lights. "Dammit," I say. "It's my brake light, I know it is." We pull over to the side of the road, and a policeman soon appears beside my window. He's early middle-aged, freshly scrubbed with a crew cut and glasses. Yes, it's my brake light, he says. He has followed us from the Trinity Site and just wants to let us know. Then he asks what we thought of what we saw.

I'm taken aback by his question, but he seems earnest. "We were just talking about it," I say. "It's pretty heavy stuff."

"Well," he says, "I didn't get out there. I just drove into the parking lot and looked at it. It's interesting, you know. I started thinking about the bomb and Hiroshima." He pauses a moment. "I don't know, maybe I shouldn't say this. But I just find myself wondering about Hiroshima. People say it ended the war and saved a lot of American lives, but I just don't know if it was right."

We talk for about ten minutes about Hiroshima, about Trinity, and about nuclear weapons in the modern world. I'm surprised at how eager he is to talk about it, and how he is clearly wrestling with the same thoughts that affected us as we drove away. Finally, almost as an afterthought, he writes us a warning and we head out. I halfway wonder if he pulled us over just so he could talk to someone about his experience there.

As we drive away, I am struck by how this "underwhelming" site can be so moving. Objectively, there is hardly anything to see, no interpretive center, no documentary film playing on an endless loop, none of the hand-holding, museum-style exhibits we associate with places of such import. Instead, the site is one of pilgrimage. And much like a religious pilgrimage, I think, its power comes from how it encourages us to internalize its meaning, to stand at a spot and consider the events that formed the world we now live in. To think about the things we take for granted, to ask questions about them, and to come up with our own answers.

"Are you glad we went?" I ask Mark as we stop for a hamburger on the way out.

"Definitely," he says.

6

Particles

Inside a glass tube, electric current heats a coil of tungsten to the point of glowing, just like a light bulb. But this current is far stronger than a bedroom lamp and will produce more than heat and light. As the current grows more energized, electrons, freed from their nucleic bonds, propel themselves from the tungsten coil into empty space.

The tube has been emptied of air, as close to a vacuum as possible, so that there are no molecules to impede the electrons' flight. They zap through the void, nearly at the speed of light, then crash into a metal plate. More heat and light erupt from the crash site, but also a group of photons moving in a tight, close pattern.

This is the X-ray.

If you place an object—say, a human being—in the path of those photons, the X-rays will pass through most of the human. And if you place a piece of halide silver film on the other side of that human, then the X-rays will collide with the grains of halide and create atoms of silver. The result is an image. The exposed film where the X-rays hit is dark; the film where the X-rays were blocked by denser objects like bones and metal are bright white.

But not all of these photons pass harmlessly through the skin and blood and meat of the human body. Some percentage will collide with molecules they encounter along the way, releasing more heat and energy, and potentially causing serious problems for the human that all these things belong to.

I was born with the bones in my left foot twisted inward and down, a condition called a club foot. It required multiple surgeries throughout my early life to cut, maneuver, and pin the bones into a place where I was no longer walking on the side or top of my foot. As such, I had many, many X-rays during my babyhood, and my mother swears that one day, after my tiny self was irradiated several times in preparation for treatment, she noticed that the technician had not taken any pains to shield my groin area from exposure. She said something to the tech, who mumbled an apology and placed a lead-lined glove over my genitals.

But, if we follow this origin tale to its conclusion, it was too late.

Because thirty years later, I got cancer.

My first inkling that my lower organs were in jeopardy came as I lay in the bath, eight weeks after the birth of my son, just before I was due to start my time as a stay-at-home parent.

To put it bluntly, and to spare you an overly personal description, at the age of thirty-one, I found a lump. After getting a second opinion from my wife (just one of the many marital duties that somehow didn't make it into the vows), I visited my doctor.

He held my testicle in his hand while I gazed awkwardly at the ceiling, stealing glances at his face from time to time. As he squeezed and rotated, he furrowed his brow and I knew something was up. Finally, he let go, met my gaze, and said, "I want you to know that I'm taking this very seriously."

My heart sank.

Four days, one ultrasound, and one MRI later, I went in for surgery to remove the tumor, and, as collateral damage, the testicle itself.

Was it the X-ray when I was baby? There's no way to prove it. But my mother's just-so story is too appealing to resist.

In 1965, Melvin Harris Briggs was twenty-five years old, though he looked younger. His sallow skin, thin frame, and chinless face gave his appearance the sort of helpless, repulsive innocence of just-hatched birds and grubs, as though he would never be equipped to survive in the world.

On Tuesday, June 8, a little after one o'clock, Briggs drove his beat-up Nash Rambler down Monroe Street in Spokane, Washington, toward the small city's downtown. A flash of blond hair attracted his attention. It was a lanky boy, about twelve years old, haphazardly hitchhiking into the city.

Melvin Briggs pulled up and offered him a ride. The boy got in.

Three days later, a landowner found the child's body—facedown, strangled, and cold, with a rope still tied around his neck—in a patch of woods behind the landowner's home.

For a week, the story held the front page of the Spokane papers. Each edition added new details to the tragedy. First the boy's identity: John Siverts, son of a prominent physician. Then a description of a "teenager" in a button-down cowboy shirt seen fleeing from the wooded area. The fact that the boy's body bore evidence of a sexual assault. And finally, the arrest and questioning of the only suspect, Melvin Briggs, identified by a judge who remembered his involvement in a similar, though nonfatal, attack on a young boy years before.

Briggs told them he had blacked out, that he had no memory of the hours of his day during which the boy disappeared. Strangely, he asked the police to drive him to the wooded patch where John's body had been found. Once there, he walked directly to where the boy's corpse had lain and started crying. "I was here," he sobbed. "I was here."

The jury sent him to prison for life.

Even Briggs thought it was probably for the best. He'd been in a mental hospital for the earlier sexual assault until two years before, and he hadn't actually wanted to leave, he said. Nonetheless, when the doctors had offered him the chance to go free, he took it. He was only human, he said.

Once in prison at the Walla Walla State Penitentiary, Briggs did well. He took advantage of rehabilitation and education programs, followed orders, kept his nose clean. On the outside, he had been a murderer, but on the inside, he was a model citizen

One day, while in the commissary, Briggs found a request for volunteers pinned to the bulletin board. It read:

> The project concerns effects of radiation on human testicular function and the results of the project will be utilized in the safety of personnel working around atomic steam plants, etc. . . . It is possible that those men receiving the higher dosages may be temporarily, or even permanently, sterilized. It should be understood that when sterilized in this manner, a man still has the same desires and can still perform as he always has. . . . [He will also] submit to surgical biopsy. (This is a simple procedure performed under local anesthesia. It is not a very painful procedure.)

Briggs had participated in one other experiment during his time in Walla Walla, and had enjoyed the experience. It was something to do to pass the time and came with perks like a bit of extra money, and the promise of a nice letter from the researcher explaining how cooperative he'd been, which would be very useful for future parole board hearings. In fact, getting selected for the test had given him something of an elevated status among the penitentiary population, even for a convicted child murderer.

Briggs contacted the warden and let him know that he was interested.

There were meetings, an assembly at which the lead scientist on the project, Dr. C. Alvin Paulsen, dark haired and friendly, greeted the men and discussed the basic experiments with them. Their testicles would be X-rayed, he said, perhaps causing some discomfort and reddened skin, but likely nothing serious, no worse than a sunburn. They would provide semen samples before and after the X-ray (giving the experiment the name "jack-off test" among the prison population). There would be, yes, a biopsy.

In exchange for $5 a month, equivalent to twenty days of the usual labor wage, added to his commissary account, Briggs agreed to allow the doctor's staff to bombard his testicles with X-rays for several minutes at a time.

Later, his $5 a month was supplemented by $10 for a biopsy. Then $100 for a vasectomy, described in layman's terms on the consent form he signed as "tying off the cords." Dr. Paulsen explained that it was necessary, because, on the off-chance Briggs ever left prison, any possible future children would have a high likelihood of birth defects.

An inguinal orchiectomy is a straightforward, if grisly, affair. Surprisingly to me, the urologist did not perform the obvious maneuver and snip his way through my scrotal sac and then sever the testicle; rather, he performed an end run around the sac, making an incision in the upper groin area and then burrowing down to where the spermatic cord enters the scrotum. Then it was just a quick yank, and the whole shebang, cord, testicle, and all, was pulled upward through the opening above the pubic bone, clamped off and then severed.

There are pictures of this procedure on the Internet, by the way. I can't really recommend that you look for them.

And that was it. Six hours after checking into the hospital, I was half-castrated and sent on my way with a few bottles full of pain medication and a temporarily lopsided gait, because somehow the removal of one of the supposed sacred implements of manhood—the amputation of the body part for which every fatherly instruction and, indeed, every instinct screams to protect at all costs—somehow this is an outpatient procedure.

As for the testicle itself, it was bagged, boxed up, and shipped out to some lab in middle America where techs cut off translucent slices, ran them through microscopes and chemical tests and determined that yes, in fact, it was cancer after all.

Dr. Paulsen, in his mid-forties during the experiments, was an expert on the human testicle, but he'd recently had a bit of an embarrassment. After an accident at the Hanford Nuclear Reservation in which a plutonium spill irradiated several workers, the AEC summoned Paulsen to consult about the possible effects of exposure on the workers' fertility. But Paulsen didn't have the expertise they were looking for.

"It became apparent to me that I really wasn't in a position—even though I had worked on male sperm production for many years—to answer their questions as to whether or not there was recovery and if so, what were the details of the recovery," he reported to Spokane's newspaper *The Spokesman-Review* in 1986.

Soon after, he set out to rectify that lack of knowledge. He attended a three-day conference in Fort Collins on the effects of radiation on the reproductive system. His longtime mentor and fellow Washington state resident, Dr. Carl G. Heller, was also attending, and the two men discussed Paulsen's experience at Hanford.

No one among the conference attendees had performed experiments on humans to determine what damage radiation could do the reproductive system. Bulls, mice, and dogs, sure, but not humans. This struck both men as counterintuitive.

"If they wanted to know about man, why not work on man?" Heller asked.

Both left the conference with a plan to explore this territory, and a population already in mind: prisoners.

The use of prisoners would hardly be unique. Since World War II, scientists had used incarcerated subjects for many experiments, from studying malaria to dosing them with psychoactive drugs. And there was a good reason for it. They weren't going anywhere, and, in the words of one researcher, they were "cheaper than chimpanzees."

So Paulsen sought funds from the AEC. Under the section of the application marked "Objective," he wrote, "To determine the dose dependent relationship between external irradiation and cell kill and inhibition of mitosis."

The funding came through to the tune of a half million dollars, and Paulsen reached out to the warden of Walla Walla State Penitentiary.

On the day of the first test, Melvin Briggs was nervous. He'd heard things about radiation, seen movies where mysterious rays turned insects and people into mad giants, heard of mutations that gave people strange powers or reduced them to simpering lumps. He'd seen a comic book where a scientist exposed to gamma rays had split into two distinct personalities, one a creature of rage and strength. He thought about his own blackouts, about the child he had killed. Would it make the terrible longings inside him stronger?

Briggs was led by a guard down a back stairway to the Walla Walla basement and into a dim storeroom converted for Paulsen's use. Briggs registered thickened walls, a partition with a slit in it, and the bulky X-ray machine itself, outfitted with a conical attachment.

Briggs disrobed and lay down on the table. Paulsen's assistant taped Briggs's penis to his leg, then placed a small cloth bag of sugar beneath his testicles, and another bag of sugar, this one oblong, over his penis. This, the assistant said, was to prevent the radiation from scattering to other parts of his body. The man then positioned the machine's cone above Briggs's groin, focusing the lighted cross hairs on his testicles.

Before the assistant left, he closed the heavy door behind him. The quiet of the room thickened.

The machine above Briggs buzzed softly. The door stayed closed. The lights remained dim. A minute went by. Then another.

Melvin Briggs lay perfectly still, as he was asked. He lay still for five minutes.

Here is what happened to Briggs's testicles as he lay there. The X-ray tube fired somewhere between 6 and 600 rads of energy in the form of photons. Those photons penetrated Briggs's scrotum, colliding with organic molecules as they journeyed through the pulp and fluid of his testicular makeup. Those collisions released more energy, disrupted molecular bonds, and pushed electrons out of their orbits. The electrons in their turn collided with other molecules. Some of them sheared off a slice of DNA, others ionized water molecules, which began careening crazily, causing more damage. Some of the cells in Briggs's testicles died immediately, others lasted a few weeks, and some showed no obvious sign of damage but harbored a secret flaw inside their DNA that would only reveal itself years later.

Briggs was one of sixty-four prisoners that Paulsen experimented on. Some were in the control group. At least one other sat beneath the X-ray machine for a full twenty minutes, receiving 400 rads.

It was all a way for prisoners to serve their country, Paulsen is reported to have said. It would be important for the armed forces to know about the effects of radiation on the human body. NASA was also interested, he said, and there was talk of a nuclear-powered airplane.

For his part, Briggs was happy to get the extra money. He spent it, he said in a later deposition, on razor blades, candy, and toothpaste.

After the surgeons removed my testicle, treatment began. This consisted, ironically, of targeted radiation administered to the lower abdomen. I showed up to the same place at the same time every day, a dingy, crowded room at the University of New Mexico's old cancer center. Most of the other patients were much worse off than me. Headscarves, sallow skin, fatigue, and a general atmosphere of hopelessness saturated the room. Once called, I would grab a red folder from the check-in desk and take it through the halls of the cancer center into a second waiting room, give it to the young woman behind that desk, and then step into a small dressing room and change into a hospital gown. Within a few moments of emerging, one of the techs would call me into the therapy chamber.

It was dim and everything happened very quickly. Before I got a good chance to look around, the techs escorted me to a narrow table and nestled me into a vacuum-formed cushion that had been molded to the contours of my buttocks. Asking questions or making small talk at this point was discouraged; these techs were not there for me but rather to prepare the machine that hovered over the slab, staring down with a mechanized, unblinking red eye. The techs pushed me, pulled me, traced X's and lines across my stomach in permanent marker, raised the table, lowered it, and eventually left.

Alone in the room, I gazed up at the machine that hung above me, attached to a long arm arching over my head and ending somewhere below the slab. It was quiet and motionless for a few moments, then sprang suddenly to life. Behind its glass lens, a light turned on; a few whirring noises emerged and then a buzz. This was the moment the radiation was released, X-rays once again propelling into my body. This time, the *intention* was that they would damage my cells, ripping into the DNA and causing them to die. Cancer cells would be unable to regrow, while normal cells would replace the fallen. Of course, there was again a risk that the X-rays could cause more cancer, but the danger from not treating the area was far greater.

I sat there trying to feel something as the invisible rays tore into me, but there was nothing. The buzz continued for perhaps thirty seconds, then the machine stopped and was quiet for a handful of seconds before it lurched back into motion. The arm turned, revolving the machine to somewhere below me. Another buzz, then quiet.

It was done.

The techs reemerged, lowered the slab, and sent me on my way. A few minutes later, as I was walking to the car, I began to feel uncomfortable. There was a touch of nausea, but more noticeable was the drug I took to combat it, which replaced most of the nausea with dizziness and fatigue. At home, I collapsed onto the couch, losing track of conversations, unable to keep up with the flow of words in a magazine article. For the next few hours, I was good for nothing but staring blankly at the computer screen or DVD episodes of television shows I'd seen many times before.

After several exposures, lesions appeared on Melvin Briggs's scrotum. Redness, tissue breakdown, sores. They lasted for weeks, and even reemerged from time-to-time years later.

For Briggs, the radiation burns and sores were painful, but it was the biopsies that hurt the most. There was no general anesthesia for the prisoners going under the knife. Instead, they received a dose of morphine—but if they had upset the prisoner orderly who administered the dose, it might be less than the stipulated amount, or simply sterile water. Even with the drug, the pain was intense enough that standard practice was for the prisoner to be held facedown, "in the event he began flailing."

Once Briggs was restrained, the doctor cut into the scrotum and removed a slice of the testicle. The pain was thick and throbbing. Another prisoner described the sensation as "like you've hit yourself on the crossbar of a bicycle, where you have an excruciating pain that starts in your testicle and radiates clear up into your side, and you have the reflex to immediately dive into a fetal position."

Outside the prison walls, though, the attitude toward using prisoners as experimental subjects was changing. Even when Paulsen had first proposed the project, there had already been rumbling concerns about "'do-gooder' organizations" interfering in their work, and the concern that the political climate would soon prevent such research ironically led to the experiment's quick approval.

Indeed, in 1969, a psychologist named Dr. Audrey R. Holliday became the head of the new research division at the Washington Department of Institutions. Holliday was well versed in human experimentation, having helped direct studies on the effects of LSD on students at the University of Washington. But when she looked into Paulsen's experiments, she saw a crucial difference: Her subjects were volunteers who did not have the threat of long prison sentences hanging over their heads. The fact that Paulsen was now requesting to expand his work by bringing a neutron generator into the prison prompted a flurry of correspondence between members of the Department of Institutions.

"I do not think we have a single leg to stand on if we allow this study to continue," Holliday wrote. Moreover, if she had been serving at the research division when Paulsen proposed his project, she said, "We never would have approved this research."

She wrote to Paulsen expressing her concerns about using prisoners for such high-risk research. He maintained that the prison was a perfect place for his experiments. She responded with sarcasm: "There is no doubt but that the prison setting is an ideal setting for this type of research. . . . I suppose concentration camps provided ideal settings for the research conducted in them."

Evoking concentration camps signaled a determination in Holliday that Paulsen couldn't argue his way out of. After lengthy memos back and forth with the University of Washington, the head of the Department of Institutions, and Dr. Paulsen, the matter came before the new Human Rights Committee for the Washington prison system. The committee made the concentration camp connection even more clear when it cited the Nuremberg Code, a set of principles of ethical research that had been articulated as part of the United States' prosecution of Nazi doctor Karl Brandt. In particular, the committee cited point 4 of the code: "The experiment should be so conducted as to avoid all unnecessary physical and mental suffering and injury."

The "do-gooders" won, and the study was officially shut down.

I was under the light for six weeks. A few weeks after that, I had recovered enough that life felt normal, with the exception of a quarterly CT scan. I was able to help raise my son, father a daughter, and live my life.

And yet I still felt unwhole, damaged, maimed. It's not an unusual phenomenon. A February 2019 medical journal article entitled "Psychosocial Issues in Long-Term Survivors of Testicular Cancer" points out that survivors often experience an "increased sense of vulnerability and uncertainty about the future, feelings of personal inadequacy, fear of social rejection and stigmatization, anxiety, depression, and symptoms of post-traumatic stress disorder." I didn't need the article to know that, but seeing it confirmed was strangely comforting.

After the committee officially shut down the experiments, Dr. Paulsen and his staff essentially abandoned the prisoners, offering no follow-up medical care. But for Briggs and many of the sixty-three other subjects, the effects of the study would continue to play out over the rest of their lives.

Briggs's lesions continued appearing on his groin, and in 1982 he developed a cyst on his penis that had to be surgically removed. Other inmates developed cancer, painful discharge, or life-long impotence. One had tumors removed from both of his breasts. Twenty-two of the subjects died before the age of sixty. Briggs and his fellow prisoners attempted to gain medical follow-ups related to the tests, but their efforts were ignored at every turn.

In 1988, the State of Oregon hired an epidemiologist named James Ruttenber to track down prisoners that had participated in similar radiation studies designed and performed by Dr. Heller, Dr. Paulsen's mentor. When Ruttenber realized that prisoners in Washington had also been subject to radiation experiments, he reached out to Paulsen to ask for a list of their names so that they could be examined and treated. Paulsen's reaction was extreme. "He went off the wall with me," Ruttenber explained to *The Spokesman-Review* in 1994. "He almost threw me out of his office. He was outraged that someone was tracking this down." When pressed further, Paulsen insisted that the prisoners had told him they did not want follow-ups, that they insisted on privacy.

In 1994, the Clinton administration's Department of Energy granted extra funds to Oregon's medical follow-up efforts. This prompted *The Spokesman-Review* to ask the Washington State Department of Corrections whether they would be implementing their own program to seek out Paulsen's experimental subjects. Scott Blonien, the state's assistant attorney general, informed the paper that it would be impossible since none of the inmates remained in prison, and there were no records of what happened to them.

Of course, Blonien was wrong, and four of the subjects were still incarcerated at Walla Walla, including Melvin Briggs. When they read Blonien's quote, they were infuriated, and reached out to the newspaper themselves. "We're mad as hell about this," one of the men, Donald Byers, said.

The Spokesman-Review spoke to the four, and Melvin Briggs specifically called out Paulsen's statement that they had not wished for medical follow-ups. "We never told him that," Melvin said.

Finally, the State of Washington formed its own initiative to find the rest of the prisoners.

Sixteen years after my surgery, it's still in my thoughts almost every day. When I bathe, I run my hand across the scar on my pelvis, a thick ridge about three inches above and to the left of my penis, ropy and numb. I worry about the possibility of the cancer returning, either to my lungs, where it would have spread next if it had been allowed to grow, or to my remaining testicle. Lung cancer, of course, carries the real possibility of death, but somehow, losing the remaining testicle scares me more. Who would I be without it?

Perhaps the most frightening aspect of the cancer was the way it came without warning, without reason. I didn't know I was at risk, any more than anyone is at risk. And even when my mother spins her stories of how it may have happened, all those decades ago—the absent-minded tech and the improvised lead shielding glove—part of me knows that she is just trying to make sense of an event that occurred entirely outside of her control. Forces, particles, chance, fate.

So here I sit, in the bathtub, touching my scar and imagining humanity itself as a collection of particles. Neutrons, protons, electrons, the whole bit, organized to maximize volition, growth, thought, love, sex, hatred, evil, anger, despair, joy, death, birth. All of it. Assemblages of particles, shooting across the earth, colliding, creating, destroying. Sometimes cancer, sometimes treatment, sometimes murder, sometimes healing.

My thoughts turn to Melvin Briggs, the imperfect victim.

If a particle entered my scrotum and damaged DNA, what blame could I give it? And if Melvin Briggs lost his mind, really couldn't remember the murder he committed, is he culpable? What are we if not a collection of forces and a smattering of chance that determines our destiny?

In 2005, Melvin Briggs took his last breath. He was still incarcerated. His cause of death is notable: lung cancer, the most common outcome for spreading testicular cancer cells. Without access to his medical records, there is no determining whether there's a relationship between the experiments and the death that took him in his sixty-fifth year, but there is cause for a raised eyebrow, at least. In the years between 1994 and his death, he had pursued a lawsuit against both Dr. Paulsen and the State of Washington, settling for an undisclosed amount in 1997.

The Spokesman-Review, the paper that had first reported on his crimes, posted a victory lap of an editorial. "No Tears over This Guy's Death," the headline read. The author, Doug Clark, went on to elaborate, "You won't find one lonely teardrop trickling down my cheek for a child-murdering piece of filth like Briggs.... Good riddance, Melvin." Oddly, the paper made no mention of the radiation experiments, despite the fact that it had first reported on Briggs's involvement in 1994.

As I consider the article, I struggle to sort out how I feel about this. Briggs had committed an unforgivable crime, and his life belonged to the state. This makes sense to me: A murderer, a child murderer especially, whether or not he remembers the crime, should be separated from the people he may harm until he will no longer have such impulses or episodes. And in our limited understanding of such crimes and approaches to rehabilitation, that day never came.

Rogue particles must be blocked.

But the photon makes no choices. People do. Whether we believe his story about the sudden fugue state or not, choice has to be one of the forces that brought Melvin Briggs to murder that child. Otherwise, we are no more than the particles that make us up. He victimized that twelve-year-old boy. But from where I'm sitting, fifty years later and utterly removed from the crime, the victim, and the perpetrator, it may as well be one more unknowable outcome, the result of aggregate forces, particles, and the whims of an infinite universe, somehow a mirror to the myriad factors that cause an X-ray to result in cancer.

And then the perpetrator faced his own victimization in the form of scientists trying to make sense of a dangerous and little-understood phenomenon.

Here is the crux. Dr. C. Alvin Paulsen decided that if prisoners had to be misled, the truth hidden from them, their vulnerable status exploited, so be it. Science, in his estimation, reigned supreme over human decency.

Is that a sort of cancer? A metastasizing cascade of harm? I wonder as my hand wanders from scar downward, feeling the remaining testicle for lumps, as I have routinely done for sixteen years.

Dr. Paulsen did not think of his work as a cancer, nor its later repudiation as a truth. He saw it as a simple shift of relative morality. "If our work was unethical, then you'd have to say that all the [federal and university advisory boards] that approved it in those days were completely unethical, and so, no, that's not true." An entire system, in other words, could not be unethical in itself.

Black men in the Tuskegee syphilis experiments, developmentally disabled children fed a radioactive oatmeal at the Walter E. Fernald State School in Massachusetts, soldiers practicing maneuvers beneath a mushroom cloud. Each subjected to tremendous risk of harm because of their value in the eyes of the society they had placed their trust in. And, of course, prisoners. All of these experiments approved by our government, all of them completely unethical.

So I turn to Melvin Briggs, perhaps the least sympathetic of the vulnerable, a man who murdered a child, who committed sexual violence upon the boy, who had offended before and who would almost certainly have offended again. If "deserving" the pain and misery of radiation burns to his scrotum were possible, then he would deserve it. Did he?

In 1974, after widespread reporting on the Tuskegee syphilis study, the federal government convened the National Commission for the Protection of Human Subjects of Biomedical and Behavioral Research, an advisory group tasked with looking into federally funded experiments involving humans. The use of prisoners was highlighted as an area of ethical ambiguity. Beyond even the ethical abuses offered in cases such as the Paulsen study, where the realities of the experiment and its possible effects were knowingly minimized and obfuscated, the group wrestled with the question of whether a prisoner, a person whose liberty has been utterly curtailed by the state, could give consent to participate in a research study at all. The commission's 1976 report, entitled *Report and Recommendations: Research Involving Prisoners,* mulled over the question of consent, particularly assertions that "prisoners cannot in principle give free consent because of the inherent nature of prisons as coercive, total institutions," as well as the morality of routinely subjecting prisoners to higher-risk experiments than those involving members of the free public, as was the practice at the time. Even financial compensation was analyzed in light of the prison's typical deprivation: Research experiments always paid well in excess of other opportunities for incarcerated people—did that create an undue element of coerciveness for those prisoners who weighed the pros and cons of subjecting themselves to the potential harm of a study?

In the end, the commission recommended that studies involving prisoners not be conducted unless they were experiments involving the nature of the correctional institution itself, or if the studies had the "intent and reasonable probability of improving the health or well-being of the individual prisoner." In 1978, the federal government used the commission's report to establish limits in biomedical testing, effectively halting experiments involving prisoners altogether.

How do I read this? Was it a triumph of good over evil? The inexorable progress of the American experiment? Was it, then, the X-ray tech remembering to put the lead apron over the subject's vulnerable body? Or was it just another unknowable event, a collection of forces and particles that shifted from one eventuality to the other, the X-rays this time missing the tissues and leaving the DNA healthy and allowed to grow?

It's beyond my understanding, like all events that take place in the greater world outside my sphere of influence, a conclusion that was reached two years after I was born but continues to resonate into my present.

And here I am, in the cooling bathtub, an unknowable collection of particles and forces, pulling the stopper and feeling the water pull away from my body, swirling into the mystery of the drain.

INTERLUDE

The Bomb

The atoms are spinning. They are spinning and unstable; waiting for a nudge; waiting for fission, literally *to split*, to break apart.

And when they do, the energy that comes boiling out from the unfathomable inner space between their component particles will be tremendous. A fiery, explosive roil that tears apart the very bonds between matter itself.

This is the basis of the bomb. Of a nuclear explosion. A fission of matter.

All elements are capable of undergoing nuclear fission and releasing the energy deep within. But two are particularly prone to it: uranium, which exists naturally upon the earth, and plutonium, its far more reactive child.

Uranium is the simpler of the two to use. Its isotope U-235, named for its 92 protons and 143 neutrons, requires relatively little encouragement. Consider this dense element; look deep at the atoms that make it up. When a stray neutron veers close to a U-235 atom, the atom briefly captures it, then becomes unstable: Its nucleus turns oblong as the forces inside it push at the bonds between particles. Then it splits into two new elements and releases its tremendous energy and shunts three more neutrons spinning outward.

And if those three neutrons happen to meet more U-235 atoms, the chain reaction perpetuates itself as long as there are enough U-235 atoms in a small-enough space to provide ample targets for the stray neutrons. When these conditions are met, the mass is labeled "critical," and the energy explodes outward as the process happens over and over again in the blink of an eye.

I find the metaphor that churns at the heart of this process inescapable. Humanity has tapped into this creative, destructive energy, and even as we seek to control it and to induce it, it reflects back at us. We bend it to our will because it is already so reflective of our wills.

The language of fission is a poetically rich environment: The original atom is a "parent," the resulting elements are "children." And the two elements whose volatility makes them perfect for an instrument of destruction, the two elements that the scientists of the Manhattan Project focused on in their creation of two bombs to drop upon Japanese cities, are uranium and plutonium, their names cribbed from the Greek/Roman pantheon. Here the metaphor attains such a degree of richness that I pull away, recoil just a little. How can anything be so perfect?

Uranus: to the Greeks, a primal father who abused his children, who locked them deep in the earth, who was eventually slain by his own son Cronus.

Pluto: the child who was consumed in turn by Cronus until Cronus met his fate at the hands of a son himself.

Interesting that these are the names chosen for the most fissile elements, for the ones whose instability leads them to explosiveness. Figures whose myths revolve around father and son.

And then, even the bombs themselves. Fat Man. Little Boy. Another paternal reference, surely.

But here is the point at which metaphors cannot hold. Two bombs falling from the clouds on two different cities, three days apart. As many as a quarter million people, mostly civilians, killed in two separate balls of fire that came roaring through the ancient cities and brought their buildings crumbling down. Human bodies vaporized, leaving only shadow on stone.

Streets filled with destruction and death. Survivors whose flesh peeled from their bodies and hung there like rags, children with blackened skin wailing by the corpses of their dead parents, early survivors who seemed unhurt at first, vomiting and growing sicker until they succumbed to a secret, invisible killer.

I can't desecrate their unburied corpses for this. My life, my family, my struggles—all vaporize before the screaming dead. The fall of those two bombs is a moment outside of craft: It was not poetry, it was not symbol, it was not myth. It simply was.

I read the accounts, watch the films, see the faces of those who witnessed it and lived, and I want to reject it wholly and completely. That's not my world, and I look out my car window on a rolling swell of piñon and juniper trees in the mountains just east of Albuquerque, a city where bombs are still transported and stored in secret hollows beneath the hills.

But it is my world and I will never escape it. My life offers an implicit endorsement: I am here because of those bombs. Reject them all I want, but my life is dependent on those two horrifying moments.

Honor them. Honor those who were killed to make this world. Human sacrifice on a mass scale to summon the lives we live. A great ugliness and evil at the heart of the twentieth century. We still argue over that moment, and will probably do so forever. It saved American lives, they say; the fighting would have gone on and on, they say; the Japanese would never have surrendered, they say.

It doesn't matter. A quarter of a million people were wiped out in two flashes as bright as the sun. No matter what else you may think, *they* didn't deserve it. It wasn't their fault. Honor them.

So I retreat now, from their tortured faces and anguished cries in my mind's eye. The uninterpretable moment settles, and I think of how the world moved on from the pain and fear and gave birth to a new mythology. The flashes filtered through the lens of popular culture. Atomic kitsch spread throughout the United States. Restaurants and hotels were named after the new power unleashed: the Atomic Inn, the Atomic Bar. Children played with nuclear bomb–inspired toys: walkie-talkies for an Atomic Chief; a target for an Atom Bomber; a science kit promising "Safe! Exciting! Real! Atomic Energy!" Cities like Las Vegas, Nevada, celebrated their role in the nuclear industry with beauty pageants for Miss Atomic Blast and parade floats in the shape of mushroom clouds.

But even there, in the heart of the neon-bedecked camp of the 1950s' adulation of the atomic bomb, there was a lurking darkness. Even housewives with kerchiefs and working husbands with ties and pipes clenched between their teeth knew that the atomic power was unstable and terrifying, that radiation spreads outward and does terrible things to people.

In the world of movies, these fears saw manifestation in black and white and Technicolor, in 3-D. Giant ants made raids from the deserts; men grew to enormous size and rampaged through cities; the atom bequeathed strange powers upon the people who were exposed to its awful mysteries; Godzilla rises from the ocean; and in the deserts of the southwestern United States, a physicist is exposed and finds himself becoming a monster.

7
Contaminant

Within each of us, oft times, there dwells a mighty and raging fury.

—Title card for *The Incredible Hulk*, 1977

In 1962, Dr. Bruce Banner, a preeminent atomic scientist, tested the first G-bomb, a device more powerful than even the mighty hydrogen bomb. Due to circumstances too convoluted to delve into here, Banner was himself exposed to the gamma rays generated by the G-bomb's explosion, and thus joined a growing throng of fictional men, women, and animals who were contaminated by a very special kind of radioactive fallout: the kind that only ever existed within the human imagination.

But even there, among the monstrous spiders and fire-breathing lizards and fifty-foot-tall women of midcentury Cold War fears, Banner stands out. Unlike them, the radiation didn't make him into an outright monster. In fact, much of the time, he is his normal, human self. But when he gets angry, he explodes into a green, ten-foot-tall incarnation of primal fury. The gamma radiation gave him a sort of cancer of the emotions, giving power and mass to his anger, turning him into a tumor of rage known as the Hulk.

Maybe it's because my own name is so similar ("Banner" and "man," nestled together so cozily), but the Hulk made an impression with me early on. I remember watching reruns of the 1970s television show with abject, horrified fascination as a small child. As an adult, I dragged my wife to see each of the films as they came out, even though most superhero movies had become an increasingly hard sell for me. In my mind, the Hulk is so much more potent than any of his Marvel or DC superhero peers. He is an archetype, fearsome and eternal.

I'm not alone in this. Most of the 1950s and '60s radioactive monster tropes are laughable today—and the fifty-foot woman was always pretty laughable anyway—but somehow the Hulk endures.

He has even outlasted the Cold War–bound myth of his origin. In numerous remakes, reboots, and relaunches, the Hulk is, yes, generally exposed to some form of radiation, but rarely does it come from a bomb. Instead, in the last two films that centered on the character, the experiment is medical in nature—the first focused on imbuing animals with regenerative abilities, and the second, ironically, on providing an immunity to gamma radiation itself. In the television series that solidified the Hulk's mass appeal, the gamma rays were released by an experiment Banner hoped would allow him to harness the great strength human beings sometimes exhibit in emergency situations.

No matter the source of the radiation, the results are always the same. Banner is overexposed and the anger he normally keeps bottled up inside of him becomes a transformative agent. When he gives in to his rage, he becomes huge and strong and uncontrollable. Cars, buildings, supervillains, and monsters are all *smashed*, and sometimes loved ones and friends are threatened.

Later, when the fit has passed, he returns to his meek, human self, horrified at his actions, living in perpetual fear of who he becomes when his anger takes hold.

The power of this fantasy is the same as that of the werewolf: Within every person there is a monster that awaits a moment of awakening—the rational mind will slip away and the primal, furious core of our most dangerous emotion will take control.

The Hulk endures because his myth, his transformation, his power and terror, are all true.

And the truth of the Hulk is this: Rage is an event, a physical response as well as an emotional one. Deep within the brain, there are two nut-shaped nodes that comprise the amygdala (from the Greek word for almond), the organ that is responsible for regulating emotions. When a person is confronted with a trigger, an incident that provokes anger, the amygdala processes the event and prompt a release of adrenaline. At the same time, blood begins to flow rapidly into the left frontal lobe, where reasoning occurs. If the frontal lobe kicks in on time, the amygdala's rage response can be averted by a sensible evaluation of the situation. If not—if the situation is an emergency for which there is no time to reason—the adrenaline will flood the body and the person will experience a full-on fight-or-flight response without the benefit of increased rationality.

Fog descends, danger lurks everywhere, action is imperative.

In other words, it's a sort of race. But not all contestants are equal. The amygdala's speed of response depends on the severity of the trigger. Being frustrated while programming an alarm clock, for instance, will produce a slower, smaller response than being punched in the face. Add to that situational variables—some people are born with a more active amygdala; others suffer brain damage that results in the same. And, like any runner who trains for the big event, the more prone to anger a person is, the more powerful the amygdala becomes and the more likely they are to experience rage, even in situations where a rational response is far more constructive.

And Bruce Banner's eyes go green.

There's no way for me to tell if my own predilection toward rage is genetic or the result of growing up in a perpetually angry household. It's a moot point, anyway. The fact is that I have, at the very least, learned to channel many of my anxiety responses into anger, defensiveness, and, yes, sometimes rage.

The amygdala is also tied to anxiety. To depression. To borderline personality disorder. I struggle with the first two. My sister is diagnosed with the third.

The amygdala. Two almond-sized and -shaped organs. Resting somewhere in the center of my brain. Pumping out hormones to decide how I feel.

That can't be right, can it? Out of all the elements beyond my control that populate this world, how can there be one at the very center of my brain? And yet, there it is.

Ask Dr. Banner. He knows. In the movies, in the TV show, in the classic comics, there are two kinds of transformation whereby Banner becomes the Hulk. The first is pure, earned anger: A bad guy throws him into a wall; aliens pit him against extraterrestrial gladiators; he is tortured while chained in a dungeon. Someone has stepped way over the line. Banner blinks his eyes and the camera zooms in on the now pale green irises. An unstoppable beast is about to kick the shit out of someone who deserves it, and we viewers feel an ecstatic rush building up in our chests. His anger is righteous and the wicked will soon be punished.

The second trigger is no less important to the myth of Hulk, but more unpleasant. Banner suffers intense disappointment: A romantic rival diminishes him before the object of his affection; a car whose tire he is replacing slips off its jack; he experiences a nightmare that twists him into emotional agony. His radioactive amygdala flares up while his frontal lobe lags behind. He squeezes his eyes shut and for a moment we hope that this time he will swallow the anger.

But we know that he won't. His eyes open wide and again the irises are pale, almost luminescent green, but there is no appropriate enemy to smite. The beast swells, walls are broken, and someone Banner loves is suddenly in danger.

In the television show, the audience is promised time and again that his innate personality prevents him from hurting anyone innocent, anyone he cares about—but how can we be sure? The Hulk is a paroxysm of uncontrollable, purely emotional violence. There is no euphoric buildup here, only fear. We know deep down that the Hulk may turn on those who don't deserve it, and that there's nothing and no one that could stop him if he did.

The latter transformation is the crux of Banner's character, and the reason he and the Hulk have achieved their popularity. Every superhero overpowers the wicked, but the Hulk is different because we know that his anger, like ours, is dangerous.

It's hard to imagine rage when you're not experiencing it. By its nature, the adrenaline response manipulates perceptions—time slows down or speeds up, peripheral vision collapses into a tunnel, certain actions disappear in the memory while others stand out, utterly, horrifyingly vivid. Knowing that I should question my own memory, I recently requested an incident report from the Seabrook, Texas, police department in order to gain as objective a record as possible of an event I experienced thirty years ago, one that I have thought of nearly every day since it happened. Surprisingly, I received not one but two reports.

The first was the one I expected:

> January 2, 1994. SUNDAY Time of occurrence: 19:11. Time of report: 19:21.
>
> Department classification: DOMESTIC VIOLENCE 01
>
> Alcohol Related: Yes. Drug related: No.
>
> UCR Classification: Assault-simple
>
> Attempt/Committed: COMMITTED
>
> UCR Type of Weapon: Hands/Fists/Feet
>
> Summary: On Sunday, 01-02-94 at approximately 1921 hours I, Officer C. Barton #217 was dispatched to 1010 East Meyer in reference to a domestic disturbance in progress. The complainant was met at a neighbor's house after she fled her residence. She reported that her husband (Suspect) struck her numerous times with hands, fist and feet. The suspect left the scene prior to official's arrival and no arrest was made at this time. Charges of class A assault were filed on the suspect.

This officer was able to briefly examine the scene while the complainant and witness gathered their personal belongings. This officer observed fragments of a shattered butter churn which covered the kitchen floor and part of dining room floor. There was also shattered glass in the dining room next to the kitchen.

VOLUNTARY STATEMENT (Not Under Arrest)

My name is Julie Hand Bannerman. . . . My husband came home and it was obvious to me he had been drinking. He has said that he has a problem with drinking and that he needs to quit. I told him that he was not someone I want to live with if he drinks and I wanted him to move out. He called me names and asked me why I was acting like this, etc. I told him I didn't think he was getting better, he appeared to be getting worse in his behavior towards me and I am sick of it. I didn't want to give him any more time to change if he was going to come home a different person.

He hit me in the head with his hand or fist knocking me to the ground, screaming at me and hitting me over and over again and kicking me. He hit me at least 15–20 times and kicked me at least 5 times. I tried to pick up a pan to hit him with to get him off me but I couldn't. I screamed for my children to call 911 and my son came into the kitchen. He told his father to quit hitting me and scuffled with him. I was still on the floor. My husband turned towards my son and threatened him and I had time to get up. He said he would "give some of this" to my son. I picked up a butter churn and tried to hit my husband with it as he went towards my son. My husband picked up a piece of the broken churn and knocked me down and tried to hit me with the broken pottery. Then I only remember he was going to the living room and my children and I went out the back door to a neighbor's house and called the police again.

VOLUNTARY STATEMENT (not under arrest)

> My name is Ty Daniel Bannerman. . . . I was eating dinner with my sister, from the kitchen I could hear the sounds of my parents arguing but thought nothing of it (It was a common occurrence in our household). I heard my father say "since when is it yours?" or something along that lines, about the house, I assumed. My mother answered with an order to leave then there was more arguing in hushed tones. Then there was a sound from the kitchen and my father raised his voice. My sister and I immediately came into the kitchen to see my mother on the ground being kicked repeatedly by my father. I snapped, grabbed him around the chest and pushed him into the oven on the side of the room. I then punched him repeatedly in the head. HE DID NOT HIT ME. He did however chase me out of the room when I stopped hitting him. He threatened to kill me. I then threw a glass at him. Meanwhile, my sister was calling the police. He then sat in his chair and my mother and sister and I left for a neighbor's house.

And so the Hulk attacked his loved one. I find myself wondering what would have happened if I hadn't been there to stop him. Would he have killed her if he hadn't been interrupted? Or would his "innate goodness," like Bruce Banner's, have stopped him before it was too late? He had shown no sign of stopping when I came into the room, kicking my mother as she squealed in pain and fear. But he allowed me to make him stop. Even then, I was surprised that he hadn't hit me back, surprised enough to write out the words on the police report in all capital letters. It was important to me, clearly, a sign that he wasn't completely gone, that he hadn't given over to the anger.

He could have attacked me, but he didn't.

He made two threats, but he didn't follow through with them.

There are details in this report that I haven't remembered in years. The broken butter churn. My father saying he would "give some of this" to me.

And details that I had never known. My mother reaching for a pan to fight him off and failing to grab it.

Reading about it on the page is like examining a static portrait, a sequence of drawings, a comic book.

In this panel, they are arguing in whispers. In the next, his fist is flying into her head. In the next, his eyes are wide and crazy, his teeth bared, his hair wild. Go back to the first. Then to the third; note the transformative moment.

The second report was the surprise. I had no memory of the incident. Even more surprising to me, this time I was named as the suspect and my mother the victim.

On February 15, a little over a month after the previous report, the same officer responded to another call from my sister. There is a brief description of the call.

> 911 DOMESTIC VIOLENCE
>
> CALLER ADVISED THAT HER 17 YEAR OLD BROTHER, TY, IS OUT OF CONTROL. HE IS BREAKING THINGS IN THE HOUSE AND IS ARGUING WITH AND YELLING AT HIS MOTHER.
>
> Scene Summary:
>
> The offense occurred inside the residence located at 1010 East Meyer. . . . This officer arrived and met with the complainant. She reported that her son became very angry after coming home from counseling. She advised that he was also upset because he was grounded and couldn't go out. She reported that he went berserk and smashed some decorations in the dining room. She advised that there were no threats made nor any physical violence.
>
> This officer spoke with the 17 years old son, Ty Bannerman, and he stated that he did break the decorations in the dining room. He reported that he was now calm and he would not damage any more property in the house. He agreed to calmly discuss the problems he was having with his mother after this officer left.

> The complainant assured this officer that he would not harm anyone in the family and stated that she would call the police if he got out of control again.
>
> This case should be classified as unfounded due to the fact that no criminal offense occurred.

Thinking back, I remember sitting on the kitchen floor while a police officer spoke to me, the same police officer who had responded to the January incident, in fact. But I do not remember the moments leading up to it, nor did I realize that it was so soon after. Looking at it now, all I can think is "of course." Of course.

One of the latest developments in the Hulk's comic book saga is Banner's discovery that he has a son, named Skaar, similarly transformed by anger, his DNA damaged by the inherited mutations from his father's original exposure. The genetic and environmental effects of anger, and the way they trickle through generations, have not gone without comment by the series writers. When the two enter into an inevitable violent confrontation, the son is a gray behemoth, mercilessly attacking Banner. With every blow, though, the Hulk flashes back on his own abuse at a father's hand. Finally, the son lies on the ground before him, shifting from monstrous form into a thin, adolescent boy. The Hulk raises his fist to deliver a final blow, but then envisions his father's face and fist in his place. He stops, and reverts to his own humanity.

In this panel, he stares at his son across the dining room. In the next, he mutters "I'll kill you," but the fire is already out of his eyes.

In the final panel, his shoulders slump forward and his face collapses into despair.

8

Oppenheimer's Children

Let the deity within you be the guardian of a living being . . .

Darkness.

Then, light.

And life comes. Silence. A gasp. A cry.

Another beginning? Over and over, beginnings after beginnings.

Here it is again. Too late to stop it. A world is born.

Again.

In 1904. In 1919. In 1941. In 1945. In 1951. In 1976. In 2008. Just as an example.

Darkness. Then. Light.

The fathers stand by, unsure of what they're feeling, unsure of their role in the creation of this new world. Unsure of their role in the world itself. Julius, Daniel, Peter, Bryon, Ty.

Imagine Oppenheimer the child, firstborn to Ashkenazi Jewish immigrants, a life of full potential and all the promise of the United States. Brilliant, but sickly, with a mind that seeks and holds.

Now, Oppenheimer the father: delicate, aloof, genius, removed. Thin, beautiful hands; intense, calculating, sparking eyes. His first child is Peter.

Now my own grandfather, Daniel, born in Washington state to an itinerant worker, a rail-riding blacksmith. Daniel becomes father to Bryon, a baby born in Los Angeles to parents who would soon move to Los Alamos. A bundle of need born early in my grandparents' marriage. Too early for both propriety and their own readiness.

Bryon as father. Trembling with excitement as he waits for his first child to come back from the hospital nursery, a turmoil of giddiness and worry, even as his eyes flick back to the Indy 500 on the black-and-white television screen hanging from the corner of the room.

And me the father, in the early-morning hours of a March day when the snow comes flurrying down in a shaft of sunlight and then stops. My son, silent for a moment, then letting out his first earthly cry. I hold him and cut his cord. I take him down to the nurse's station while my wife sleeps. They give him his first bath there, gently washing the waxy vernix off of his pinkening skin while I stand by, and then when he is out and wrapped in his towel, I brush a finger along his brand-new cheek.

The body and its parts are a river, the soul a dream and a mist . . .

Now there's a voice.

Marcus Aurelius, last emperor of the Pax Romana and well-meaning father. Aurelius's *Meditations* are on the floor by my bed, a font of words on self-control, discipline, and governance. A Stoic, to whom passions should remain in thrall to sensible thoughts.

A father who lived two thousand years ago, whose finger must have brushed his own son's cheek. Whose words, the same that I read, perhaps echoed in his child's ears.

Every rational animal is his kinsman, and to care for all humans is according to human nature. . . .

We are made for cooperation, like feet, like hands, like eyelids, like rows of the upper teeth. To act against another then is contrary to nature; and it is acting against one another to be vexed and turn away.

Never value anything as profitable that compels you to break your promise, to lose your self-respect, to hate any man, to suspect, to curse, to act the hypocrite, to desire anything that needs walls . . .

When the anxiety rages in my brain and body, I pick up *Meditations* and read his millennia-old thoughts to bring my own into rein.

But there is a flaw with Aurelius. A glaring chink in his armor of philosophic self-control, and a warning for any father. His son, Commodus.

Peter Oppenheimer was born in 1941, before the Manhattan Project, in a time of turmoil. A world war raged, secret plans were coming together, and his parents were drinking.

Some historians have suggested that Peter may have had a learning disability. There are rumors that his mother, Kitty, was often frustrated to the point of rage in raising him. But these rumors and interpretations perhaps all comes down to one fact: Peter was, and is, a whole other person than his genius father. He lived his life, separate from his parents, grappling with the legacy of his famous, infamous name, in his own way, and having his own children.

Peter Oppenheimer was a craftsman before he retired. A carpenter. He had trouble—anxiety, pain, alienation. Like all of us.

He won't talk to you about it. He lives in Santa Fe now.

My own father, shortly before he died, said, "I thought you'd be more like me." He didn't say it in a cruel way, or a disappointed way, but with a touch of bewilderment, maybe wonder, in his voice. His brown eyes were soft then. Here I was, somehow, a whole other person.

How does that happen, anyway?

Straw-colored hair, gray-green eyes, a heaviness about her personality; she is a serious person who is weighed down by things. She worries, that's clear.

And why not? Her last name is a reminder of an ever-present threat looming over the world. She is J. Robert Oppenheimer's granddaughter, Dorothy Oppenheimer Vanderford.

"When someone finally uses a bomb," she says, after we've placed our orders at a Boulder City, Nevada, diner, "it will trickle down through the family name." She's telling me how she worries about her children, who, at this age, are only tangentially aware of the importance of the name Oppenheimer. "They'll have to deal with it."

Dorothy speaks in inevitabilities. "When" someone uses the bomb. Not "if."

"I really don't want Trump to be the one. And I worry about that, I really do."

She tells me, though not in explicit words, that she feels guilt for not working to counter the effects of her grandfather's legacy. She feels powerless, she says, helpless. "I'd have to give up my life," she offers as explanation. "I'd have to focus on that exclusively. And I want to live and be my own person."

Her brother is the guardian of the Oppenheimer legacy, she says, positioning himself at the forefront of inquiries. She has always been more ambivalent. The first time she became aware of the importance of her name was when she was a child in elementary school. "Your dad invented the bomb," the boy said, getting key facts wrong in the way only a child can. "It's all your fault!"

When she married, she changed her name with relief. Dorothy Oppenheimer became Dorothy Vanderford.

But now she's not so sure. It's not something she can escape. The legacy is something that will always be there, under the surface, waiting to bubble up.

Is there anything more complicated, wonderful, vast, and difficult than parenthood? It is the awesome touch of eternity, to know that your choices will ripple down through generations. That your choices will *be* generations.

Of course, you sacrifice yourself. Every divine act requires a sacrifice, and what is more profound than the sacrifice of self?

But it is not comfortable. It is frightening. Children carry death within them.

To be correct, it must be death and life that wells inside of them, like an elixir. My children are a continuation of my genes; they have me in their very being and will bring that legacy to a world I will never know. But at the same time, their youth and growth are an emphatic reminder that this world is moving away from me, that it will continue long after I am gone.

I see them reflecting me, but also growing into themselves. My sixteen-year-old son, Bryce, with brownish-blond hair, the same color mine was when I was a child, but also a deep, abiding love for reptiles and science that I never knew. My thirteen-year-old daughter, Bronwyn, laughing at my dumb jokes, adding her own, her eyes the same brown as my father's, but kind and tender; her hands are steady and artistic in a way I always wanted mine to be. I have nurtured my children to be their own people, but also to carry my hopes into the world.

But who am I to do so? My grasp of their ongoing existence is tenuous at best, my take on the world nothing but a puzzle box of limitations and shortsightedness.

Try to be good, I tell them. Try to see the good in others. Understand that you will make mistakes and that there are simply some things you cannot control. Hope that it all works out. Oh, and recycle.

One thing here is worth a great deal: to pass your life in truth and justice, with a benevolent disposition even to liars and unjust men.

Aurelius the father took his own child, Commodus, and raised him with the Stoic values that had helped him through hardship, pain, and power. Then, seeing his son as heir apparent, he elevated Commodus to the position of co-emperor at a young age so that he could learn by watching his father and by doing the business of rulership himself. They were a team, father and son, ruling together, traveling the empire together, even entering the Eleusinian Mysteries together, and Rome's future seemed in good hands.

But then Aurelius died of an unknown affliction at the age of fifty-eight. Commodus, now eighteen years old, assumed the mantle of power.

"I changed my last name when I got married partly to separate from that identity," Dorothy says while I put away another forkful of eggs and chorizo. "Now I kind of wish I hadn't. Because it *is* my identity."

You can't escape your lineage, even if, because of adoption, divorce, or other separation, you actually know nothing at all about one or both parents, even if you never learned your father's name; it's there in your genetic code, hardwired. Legacy is a shining thread, stretching back and dividing through your parents, dividing again, again, until it is a woven tapestry of identity all funneling down to you, the ultimate end of all history.

That tapestry is you, maybe more important than anything you'll ever do in your life, and more consequential to what you are and will leave behind. And if you have your own children? The end shifts, your identity joins the threads and knots, nothing more than another waypoint in a garment whose shape you will never know.

Sometimes I feel like it's too much, being part of this world. Too much responsibility. An action leads to a reaction, leads to ripples and explosions and doubt and death. I am sorry to say I wrestle with the urge to leave the world. To sidestep the responsibility. Why not? It's an inevitability.

But, by the same token, why rush? Death will get to you soon enough.

It's a constant war. Inside me, the balance shifts to one side or another.

My father struggled with mental illness and addictive behaviors. He didn't know how to be a father (who does?). When his death came for him, lying in bed, racked with pain, and my sister held his hand and the darkness closed in, was it a relief? To know that here it ends, there is no more damage to be done? The choice is beyond you now, and there are no more mistakes to be made?

Or was it instead regret? His chances to fix, to repair, were fading out with his vision.

I know the answer: It echoes that slightly shifting line inside me, the border between the desires for life and death. Of course, for him, it must have been both. And more. Life is no simple, linear expression. It's a tangled mess of contradiction and murky glass, a mélange of disparate elements churning and coagulating. I suppose there was no single thought that came to him as he lay dying. Fear and hope and a medley of anger and relief.

I can only hope that the cessation of those feelings was a moment of peace before the end.

And I am his age now: forty-three. What used to seem an ancient number, now a simple fact of the every day.

I calculate. When exactly did he die? He was born in August and died in April. He was forty-three years and eight months. I was born in April. If I died at the exact same age as him, I think as I count on my fingers, I would be dead in December.

It's December as I write this.

Toni was Oppenheimer's second child. She was born at a difficult time. They were all difficult times. They *are* all difficult times. But she was born while her father worked on the atomic bomb, the greatest trouble to ever afflict the world. Early on, her mother left for a period of months, taking Peter with her. J. Robert Oppenheimer, overwhelmed with, well, everything, left Toni in the care of a family friend, Patricia.

He was not a father of warmth and closeness, but a father who regarded children as one more obstacle put forward by the world to take a man away from his thoughts, his ideas, his work.

"Toni has grown very fond of you," Robert said to Patricia during one of his infrequent visits to see his child in 1945, tamping tobacco into his ever-present pipe. "Would you, perhaps, want to adopt her?"

Patricia was silent for a moment, reaching for the word. "No, Oppy," she said. "No. I don't know what to say. But no."

Robert nodded and lit his pipe. Toni nuzzled into the crook of Pat's elbow.

A child is an insurmountable responsibility. A responsibility literally for life. Your life, the child's life, and the lives that come after. A drop into a pond, ripples spreading out, intersecting with other ripples, sometimes fading, sometimes growing, reaching the shore, pulling dirt in, depositing flotsam, another small soldier in an endless process of change.

Why not let someone else take her? Someone else could let the droplet fall. Let it be their hands that release it and make the ripples their responsibility.

But no. You can't. The child is yours. Even when others take it, raise it, love it, nurture it, the child is yours and will always be yours.

But why would he not want to surrender this small responsibility? His third child was on the cusp of being born and its ripples would be profound.

The words are well known. "Now I am become Death, the destroyer of worlds." Did he say them aloud or only think them? Either way, as he peered out from his bunker to the blinding fire that moments before had been a New Mexico plateau, he looked on his child with both awe and fear. How could any mere human baby match that terrifying spectacle? And the world shuddered on its axis.

To create a child of your own design and for that design to be the greatest mass murderer in human history, the Bhagavad Gita quote rattling around in his mind and every anecdotal retelling of the Trinity test forever after, was right. He was, at least in that moment, Death.

And his child was worse.

That which is not good for the hive is not good for the bee either.

At first, Commodus tried to be a good ruler, or at least generally benign. He really wasn't even that interested in power, content to pursue his passion for sport and combat while his chamberlain and advisers ran the empire.

But then the knives came, the plots grew thick around him, and he learned he was vulnerable. But where his father had somehow persevered through the bad times to continue to rule with an even hand, the threat of raised daggers pushed Commodus further and further until, finally, he broke.

He dismissed his father's advisers and rejected his father's philosophies. He now reveled in his unquestioned power. He declared himself, first, the incarnation of Hercules. Then the reincarnation of Rome's founder, Romulus himself. He ordered that the twelve months now carry his own twelve names, most of which he had given to himself: Lucius, Aelius, Aurelius, Commodus, Augustus, Herculeus, Romanus, Exsuperatorius, Amazonius, Invictus, Felix, and Pius. Then, he renamed the city: Colonia Lucia Annia Commodiana.

He knocked heads off statues and replaced them with his own face. He staged fights against the wild beasts of Africa and rigged them so he would be victorious. He lashed out at his enemies, real and imaginary, sometimes slaughtering whole families for some perceived slight. He built himself another statue and announced that he had personally killed twelve thousand men.

Eventually, one of his servants strangled him in his bath.

If even the wisdom of Marcus Aurelius was not enough to ensure a noble child, then what hope do the rest of us have?

Imagine me, the father. Two children now. Growing up in this world I can't understand. Somehow worse than it's always been, but also somehow no worse than it's always been. Our president threatens to blow another country to smithereens and asks whether nuclear weapons could be effective for stopping hurricanes in their tracks. My children sleep uneasily, all too aware of the tension in the world.

What can a parent do but try for the right thing and hope that it makes a difference?

But how strange also to be a child. The parent is the model and the source of life. A god, hideously flawed. You will always live in their shadows, and when they are gone, they will haunt you as you try to make sense of them.

There are no books written about Peter and Toni, for they did not end a world war only to unleash hell upon the earth. They struggled, suffered, fell in love, did all the human things that are worthy in and of themselves. But their story is too much like our stories, maybe. Too much for me to drive up to Peter Oppenheimer's home in Santa Fe and knock on his door, to hound him until he talks to me about what he doesn't want to talk about.

And then there is this: One of radiation's effects is the literal breaking of DNA, the ionization invading the molecules of our very selves, pushing an electron from its orbit, changing the warp and weft of us in ways that may not even be visible until we pass it along to our children, or they pass it along to theirs.

An atomic bomb, then, singes our landscape and ourselves, writing its detonation into our bodies. How many of us carry this new text within our bodies? The cloud of fallout from Trinity traveled far, even as far as Rochester, New York, two thousand miles away, where film at the Kodak headquarters fogged from exposure. And in the seventy-five years since, at least 520 more nuclear tests, almost all of them more powerful than Trinity, have sent their radioactivity into the atmosphere. Could any of us have escaped some level of contamination?

Oppenheimer made us all his children on that day in 1945.

Poor Toni. Of the two siblings, she was the steady one for so long. Shy, they say, and one who sought compromises in the various turmoils that rocked the family. But an anger grew in her. She resented her mother, and her father's death by cancer in 1967 hit her hard.

She sought to work for the United Nations as a translator. But the FBI would not give her clearance. Her dead father was a suspected communist. Her background was suspect.

She retreated then to the family's cottage on the Caribbean island of Saint John. Her marriages failed. So did her restaurant. She spent all her time on the island, alone. A recluse. One day her ex-husband came to check on her. He found her in the home's patio, hanging from a beam, dead at thirty-two.

He knew. He knew from the moment Trinity detonated. He knew before. He knew what he had unleashed on our world. There were parties in Los Alamos that evening after the test, but Oppenheimer's mask was all too easy to see through. He was worried. A fellow scientist heard, through the revelry and music and dancing and laughter, Oppenheimer muttering to himself. He was saying, "Those poor little people, those poor little people."

Hiroshima. Then Nagasaki.

The war was over, but bodies burned. The seemingly healthy died suddenly of an unknown sickness. The cities were waste.

At the news of the first bomb, Frank, Robert's brother, held his head in horror at the thought of all the destruction. Robert was, an FBI informant reported, a nervous wreck.

After the war, he resigned from directing Los Alamos. At the ceremony, he said, "The time will come when mankind will curse the names of Los Alamos and Hiroshima."

Then, in a meeting with President Truman in the Oval Office, Oppenheimer cried out that he had blood on his hands.

"I don't want to see that son of a bitch in this office ever again," Truman told his secretary after Oppenheimer left.

Like clockwork, on December 26 I wind up in the emergency room with chest pains, visions of my father's prone form inescapably flooding my mind. Is this how he felt? I think as my arm throbs, as my head grows lighter. I was playing a board game with my daughter, when I brought my head down. "What's wrong?" she asked. I could only think of my mother's words, describing an incident shortly before his death: "He rested his head on the table, white as a sheet."

Panic and anxiety. All I can think about was my father's death at the exact same age I am now. The staff gives me an EKG, a chest X-ray, and blood work.

And then I sit, for three hours until the man seated next to me gets into an altercation with the nurse.

"Are there any rooms available?" he asks.

"Yes, we have rooms," she answers, then continues, "but they're all full now."

A few more exchanges and the man begins to curse at her, loudly.

That's enough for me. I figure if they haven't called me back to see a doctor after three hours, then I'm probably not in any mortal danger. I leave.

I'll see my primary care doctor in two weeks, but the feeling of imminent demise has gone.

Just a visit from a ghost, I suppose.

Dorothy is telling me about her name change again. "For years, I sought anonymity, but now I feel responsibility," she says. "Social responsibility. Ethical responsibility for something that, you know, I wasn't alive for, so it's not really anything to do with me.... So that led to feelings of guilt and sometimes shame, but also pride."

She laughs, "There's a certain arrogance. I come from this completely smart grandfather. Somehow, he was smarter and better than the average person. And so I must be too. I've had lots of difficulty adapting to the world."

I recognize this. The entitlement my own father seemed to feel because he came from the geographic brain trust of Los Alamos. The entitlement my uncle seems to also feel, the idea of being somehow elevated above the world. The entitlement I feel as well, my difficulty finding a place in society and professional work.

"But honestly, when I think about that legacy," she continues, "I think about the bomb. The family legacy really is the legacy of the bomb. And I feel overwhelmed and powerless."

She pauses, her fork poised above her plate. Then she shrugs. "I feel afraid."

It is easy to place so much blame on one man, even natural. He was the genius, after all, the one who made the bomb happen. But he was not alone; 130,000 people worked on the Manhattan Project, though most of those were unaware of the full scale of the enterprise. A team of several hundred scientists lived and worked in Los Alamos in full knowledge of their end goal. Numerous members of the government and military stood behind it and made it happen. And untold numbers of functionaries, bureaucrats, scientists, engineers, and politicians support it to this day.

But Oppenheimer is so convenient, with his gimlet eyes and quiet, conflicted intensity. One man who encapsulates the contradictions of the bomb. The fascinating science behind it, the fear of not having it, the fear of having it, the horror and pain of power and violence. And that he knew he was wrong, how perfect is that? The remorse of the now sober parent, crying and asking forgiveness for the blows he rained down and the rending words he screamed out.

If it were only him. Then we could forgive him and be done with it.

My son is sixteen now. My daughter thirteen. I wish I could make sense of this world for them, give them the wisdom and answers they need to survive and thrive within it. But I can't. I don't even have a basic philosophical framework, like Marcus Aurelius, though it didn't seem to have done Commodus or Rome much good. I have lived in confusion and struggle; the world is beyond my understanding. I wish that weren't the case, but it is.

In a perverse way, I almost find this fact comforting. We do what we can with the time we are given, and the answers I have found and lessons I have learned will not necessarily help or hinder my children. This world will be theirs and whatever help I can offer, whatever example I can provide, they will have to be their own people and find their own way. The most I can do is say to them, yes, I went through it too. No, I don't know how to make sense of it. But I went through it, and so did everybody else. I made a slight impact, hardly perceptible, in the way things are. I don't know for good or evil, but I hope for good on balance.

My son, with his wild hair and rail-thin frame, will ultimately have to find his own way. My daughter, with her soft, expressive eyes and inquisitive mind, will ultimately have to find her own way.

What would Marcus Aurelius have done and thought if he had seen the destruction his son wrought upon Rome? Would he have castigated himself, bent over double in pain at the thing that had come from him and slashed a scar in the flesh of his city? Perhaps. But maybe Commodus served as an ultimate affirmation of his father's philosophy, that you can do what you can with the time you are given, strive for what you feel is right, but that the world itself will always remain beyond you, that your fellow humans are beyond your control, that maybe what matters is the intention, because the result is too often unknowable.

And then, back to Oppenheimer. Was his intention enough? Was the devastation outweighed by his hope?

I honestly don't know.

At the follow-up appointment, I sit in the examination room waiting for the doctor. I know I didn't have a heart attack, and I feel stupid for being here.

There's a mirror across the room from the chair I'm sitting in and the reflection catches my eye. Here I am, forty-three years old, a father to two children. Bearded, balding. I hold my hands on the top of my head, covering up my thinning hair, bringing my forehead up farther.

There he is.

My father looks back at me.

I'm him. Twenty-six years after his death, somehow me still, but also him.

It's frankly chilling, and there's a lump in my throat as I take my hands down from my head, allowing my sandy-brown hair to appear where his head was only bald skin.

He's still there, though, and I can't take my eyes away until the doctor comes in to tell me that I didn't have a heart attack, that my EKG and blood tests were normal, that my heart is still strong.

Good-bye, ghost, I think, as I leave the clinic.

And Commodus, in the bath, his servant's strong hands clenched around his neck, holding him under the water. The panic is subsiding; he stops struggling. A moment of clarity as he realizes it is too late, that he is going to die.

Does he think of his father? Does he remember Aurelius's words? Or does he simply let go, with relief, taking in a final moment of freedom before oblivion . . .

Do not live as if you had endless years ahead of you. Death overshadows you. While you're alive and able—be good.

INTERLUDE

Kelley

New Year's Eve, 1958.

He'd been called away to the DP Site to mix a batch of plutonium, despite the fact that he was supposed to be at a party. But Cecil Kelley knew his duty. He grumbled a bit to himself, but it was something that had to be done. Inside the plutonium separation room, with its rows of chemical tanks, he flipped the switch to start the mixer for the vat of solution.

But something was wrong.

There was a groan from the mixing blades, as though they had gotten stuck. He pursed his lips and flipped the switch to its off position. The noise stopped.

He pulled a stepladder across the concrete floor to the huge vat, then climbed it to peer through the viewing port and into the mixing chamber itself. There was nothing obviously wrong with the viscous liquid inside. Frowning, he reached over to a switch on the tank itself, and toggled it. With a start, the blades began to turn again, smoothly this time. A vortex formed in the center of the liquid contents. He allowed himself a smile. Whatever was wrong had been resolved.

And then

And then

And then

A blue explosion of light

a metallic clang

a force flung him from the ladder

his head struck the ground.

Somehow, he pulled himself up. Somehow, he reached for the switch again, somehow turned it off.

And then his skin began to burn.

9

Exhibition

Cecil Kelley, thirty-eight years old. Killed by a lethal dose of plutonium radiation. As the body lies on the table in the Los Alamos Medical Center, it all seems so still, but no—inside, death is unlocking another life that has too long been waiting in the shadows. The cells of the body, no longer fed by blood, no longer given oxygen from breath, no longer able to defend themselves from the bacteria and microbes that have been eager to feed on them for the nearly four decades of Kelley's life, begin to rupture. Enzymes tear down the once-living walls that held them back from the rest of the body's tissues. In the stomach, the microorganisms that have called his gut home and worked so kindly to help Kelley digest the organic compounds he needed to survive have already noticed the change. At first, hesitant, but then in a greedier and greedier frenzy, they turn to the organic compounds they know best, the inner flesh of the human body that sheltered them, that shared the full feast of life with them, and now offers itself as a final course.

At the same time, a man in a protective full-body suit is preparing to autopsy Kelley. Over the course of the next few hours, Kelley's body will be dismantled, his parts weighed, analyzed, and measured to determine exactly what destruction the plutonium has wrought.

The man begins by cutting into the skin on Kelley's chest.

I remember Dr. Sherman as a kind man, smiling beneath his wide mustache as he went over the various options with my parents. I didn't pay much attention as they discussed recovery time or the surgical breaking of bones or Sherman's estimation of the need for more surgeries when I got older; I preferred, instead, to examine the landscape of plaster bumps on the cream-colored examination room walls, but my ears pricked when the doctor mentioned "a small potential for amputation." I'd had five surgeries already, but after each, the bones in my left foot began to twist themselves back into the classic "clubbed" formation, giving me both a noticeable limp and pain when walking.

He must have noticed my suddenly fixed attention, as he then addressed me directly. "That means . . ." he began, looking for the right words to explain the concept to a nine-year-old, "we might have to surgically remove your foot. It's a small chance, but something to bear in mind. You would, of course, be given a prosthetic . . . a false foot that would let you walk and even run."

I thought about it for a moment, then asked, "But what would you do with my real foot?"

"Hmm . . ." the doctor's expression turned solemn. "Do you have a dog?"

They didn't wind up amputating my foot—just another surgery that didn't quite do the trick—but the doctor's words stuck with me. Not the grotesque punch line, but the idea of my left foot being removed from my body. In my imagination, after the amputation I would be sent home with the foot floating in a jar. I would keep it under the bed, maybe in the closet. Show it to friends. I already felt that the foot, with its malformed shape, its slight throb of ache, and its intermittent needs for medical attention, was somehow apart from me—a chunk of myself I wouldn't mind getting rid of. But still, you know, keeping around for old time's sake.

As for the dog, my mother bought him a squeaky toy in the shape of a human foot, but he was old, and hardly played with it. Within the year, he had died. My father wrapped up his body in a black trash bag, and carried the stiff, suddenly anonymous mass into the woods behind the house, where we buried it. Soon after, the woods were torn down and the earth tilled up to make way for a housing development. I suppose a jumble of dog bones and plastic bag now lies beneath a cheap suburban house in the Lake Mija neighborhood of Seabrook, Texas.

Seven years later, it was my father who died, suddenly and unexpectedly of a heart attack. My mother and sister picked me up from school and when we got home, he was long gone, carried away by the EMTs that had stormed the house that spring morning. All that was left was a small drop of blood on the bedroom carpet from when a tech had inserted a syringe during the last failed effort to save his life. He was cremated, and I never saw the body.

I read somewhere that when a pet dies, the owner should allow the other animals of the household a moment to see the corpse of their companion. A sniff, a gentle nudging perhaps, the theory goes, and they will understand and accept what has happened. It's one of those things that people believe on faith because it makes a certain amount of sense, but there is no research behind it. A Google search doesn't turn up anything in the way of hard facts or statistics, but it does turn up anecdotes of dogs, frantic and whimpering, racing through a suddenly quieter house in search of their lost friend; bereft mares nosing the pile of straw where their departed foal once slept; cats mewling and pacing in a doorway, awaiting the return of their feline housemate.

Is it perhaps the same for people? Of course, *we* can be told of a death, and the conscious mind, at least, can be made to understand. But somewhere below, in the dark places of the brain, the sudden absence remains inexplicable. He was here. Now he is not. Where did he go?

He left us for another family. He was a secret agent and had to go on a last-minute mission that he couldn't tell us about. He just got lost, somehow, he doesn't know where, but lost for a long, long time. But he's back now, and he's sorry for leaving, and he won't do it again. The dreams start out comforting, but then they ache; then they are angry. Searching, pawing, howling; the animal of my subconscious pacing the corners of the mind.

As the man cuts into Cecil Kelley's chest, fluid spills from the incisions, a mixture of saline, blood, and pulp from the heavy course of hydration Kelley was subjected to during his last hours of life. With the Y-incision complete, the man pulls the skin on the chest and abdomen back, placing the top flap over Kelley's face. He slices into the cartilage connecting Kelley's sternum to his ribs, then he takes a saw to cut through a portion of the ribs and sternum themselves. Next, he removes each organ in turn and places it in a sink beside the table. Soon, Kelley's body cavity lies empty.

And now, a shift away from the autopsy and away from my foot, to a third place where a man they call Dr. Death smiles at us. Dr. Death wears a black fedora, typically cocked at a rakish angle. There are, to my knowledge, no photographs taken of him since the 1980s in which the fedora does not perch atop his delicately featured and archetypically Germanic face, whether he is dressed in a darkly debonaire and impeccably tailored suit or in the surgeon's motley of scrubs and mask. It is his trademark, an homage, he has told interviewers, to Rembrandt's oil painting *The Anatomy Lesson of Dr. Nicolaes Tulp*.

Since he has offered this painting to us as an insight into his world, let us consider it. Painted in 1632, it is a hazed study of a Dutch surgeon's public dissection lecture. Tulp, a prominent anatomist, stands bedecked in black cloak, broad-brimmed hat, and white collar, pulling apart the sinews of a cadaver's arm with a stage magician's aplomb as an audience of leering figures leans in with ghoulish fascination. Notably, only two of these figures are surgeons. The others are noblemen who have paid for the privilege of attending the lecture. Rembrandt's shadows settle over them, pooling especially upon the eyes of the corpse.

Of course, Dr. Death is not our fedora and art enthusiast's given name. It is rather a title bestowed upon the seventy-nine-year-old Dr. Gunther von Hagens by the European media, who have both hounded him and reveled in his sensational exploits for over two decades. But the name is fitting: He is a doctor, and death is his domain.

His seminal moment came in the mid-1970s at a lunch counter in Heidelberg, Germany. Von Hagens had completed his medical education only a few years before, and had by then realized that he was not interested in living people but rather the bodies they left behind. That afternoon, on a lunch break from his position at the local university as a research assistant investigating new ways to preserve human tissue, he stood at the aforementioned counter and waited for a sandwich. As he watched, the worker cut the meat into thin sheets with a deli slicer, and inspiration struck. Why not, he thought, apply the same process to a human kidney or other organs? Then take the slices and encase them in sheets of plastic? This would allow researchers to handle them, share them, and utilize the same slices over and over, whereas at the time, students and researchers were forced to use a new, fresh organ for each occasion. Perhaps, he thought, even *infuse* the slices with the plastic somehow, and keep the decay process at bay forever?

Upon his return to the lab, he requested funds for a deli slicer of his own and began to experiment with different methods of preserving tissues in plastic. By 1977, he had perfected his process, which he called "plastination." As he had predicted that day at the lunch counter, penetrating the thinly sliced organic tissues with a polymer such as silicone rubber allowed them to be preserved indefinitely; what's more, the tissues were dry to the touch, and could be manipulated and positioned. He applied his process first to organs, then moved on to limbs, and then to full human bodies.

Imagine Dr. Death leaning over that first whole human corpse, preparing it for the plastination process. In a grim coincidence, it is actually the body of a close friend of his, a fellow surgeon who donated his body to science.

He begins by cutting away the skin.

The man now measures and then dissects each of Kelley's organs in turn: lungs, heart, liver, spleen, stomach. The stomach and the liver show the most damage from the criticality accident that knocked Kelley off of his ladder and onto the ground in a burst of blue light. The liver is dark and swollen. The stomach and intestines are hemorrhaged and filled with fluid. The man in the suit now takes a sample of bone marrow. He is surprised to find that it is not dark red and viscous, but rather a watery red mixture that seeps and pools.

Now, some half a century later, Gunther von Hagens is a multimillionaire, and I am standing in a dilapidated convention center hall in Albuquerque, surrounded by plenty of bodies and body parts to look at. It is, perhaps, too convenient to ascribe the morbid impulse that brought me here to a lingering, unresolved wish to find, even after all these years, the last remnants of my father, but I cannot help thinking of him as I examine one of the de-skinned, posed human corpses that make up the touring show *Bodies: The Exhibition*. Oddly, I am not thinking of him because this corpse has inspired thoughts of death. It is actually the opposite: The object in front of me seems removed from both life and death, somehow floating free of the human existence it once lived as well as the conclusive silence of the grave where, had things been different, it may have rested. As I peer into its ambiguous expression (slackly open mouth, neither smiling nor frowning, eyebrows raised in a slight hint of surprise), I am trying to find some way to connect this peculiarly inhuman mannequin to the real, dead people I have known.

It is one of the strangest things I have ever seen. Its glass eyes gaze blankly from a passive, skinless face; the eyelids, the curved ellipse of eyebrows, the flesh of a nose and lips like thin twists of modeling clay are all that remains of its identifiable features. The rest of it is a mass of naked musculature, red and textured somewhere between beef jerky and stretched, aged rubber.

In the hall, more of these skinless humans stand raw and close enough for visitors to touch (but *please don't touch*, warn the repeated signs), posed into the same approximations of life that you see in the gauzy photos in insurance brochures and slow-motion montages in psychiatric drug ads: kicking a soccer ball, throwing an Olympian discus, or, like the one I am currently inspecting, clutching a football. The musculature of each is exposed, in some places peeled back and pinned to highlight a certain bone structure or an organ. Music, new age and atmospheric, plays in the background; soft lights shimmer in abstract designs on the cracked and stained convention center floor; flat-screen monitors hang in front of red partitioning curtains, playing an endless loop of anatomy-oriented CGI animation as a friendly, authoritative narrator offers pearls of wisdom like "You only have one body . . . One *amazing* body . . . Without your body, you would be nothing at all."

It's the middle of the morning on a weekday, and surprisingly I am one of a sizable crowd of attendees. There are a number of businesspeople, name tags still pinned to their chest as they kill an hour or so before the next event at their conference; many families, sets of parents and teenagers mostly, but at least one with a child approximately age ten; and a handful of medical professionals or students still wearing scrubs.

Milling through the hall, waiting for clusters of people to move so I can look at the specimens, I wonder why so many of us have made it here on a day when Albuquerque museums are typically empty.

Maybe there is a hint in the show's marketing. Although the exhibition's producers argue that its purpose is educational, the advertisement flyers that litter the counters of local coffee shops, the billboards that loom over every major road in town, and the posters taped to store windows seem to be making an appeal that has little to do with offering a chance for the general public to learn about anatomy. *Bodies: The Exhibition*, the ad copy proclaims, *FEATURING ACTUAL* ***HUMAN*** *BODIES*. In case you missed it, the "**HUMAN**" is in bold, just above the image of one of the show's flayed-cadaver stars. This event is not about education. It is about gawking at corpses.

And that is certainly why I am here. There is no denying my own ghoulish streak; things that offer a glimpse of the dead have always fascinated me. In every place I've lived, I visit the graveyards, seeking especially along the ragged edge of the old cemeteries for the overgrown and dilapidated plots, for shattered headstones and sunken ground from long-collapsed coffins, for crypts and mausoleums that were erected as monuments for eternity but have now lapsed into neglect and forgetfulness, their doors pried open by vandals, their human remains jumbled and scattered. When my wife and I taught English in the Czech Republic, weekend after weekend I dragged her off to see the country's grisliest sights—the Sedlec Ossuary, where some seventy thousand skeletons have been assembled into pyramids and coats of arms and chandeliers and monstrances in a tiny underground vault, and to the Church of St. James in Prague, where a purported thief's mummified arm hangs from a hook on the wall, a testament to the vengeful and miraculously vicelike grip of a statue of Mary. I am drawn to these sights, these memento mori that have escaped, or were never subject to, my culture's inclination to hide the dead away from view.

As I watch the visitors mill around a room of plastinated bodies, it is clear that I am not alone in my hunger for tangible reminders of death. Can it be a coincidence that as our cultural separation from the persistent fact of death grows more stark, movies grow increasingly gory, that the top-selling teenaged fantasy novels revolve around love affairs with vampires, that some form of collective anxiety is expressed through a never-ending barrage of movies, novels, video games, and comic books where the dead rise en masse around us like a suppurating dam burst? That touring exhibits promising "actual human bodies" rake in millions of dollars annually?

The man in the protective suit now takes Kelley's organs and places them, one at a time, in a whole-body counter, a chair-like device fitted with Geiger counters and Nixie-tube readouts that analyzes gamma radiation. After the organs have been measured, Kelley's empty body is placed within the counter. The combined measurements show that Kelley has been exposed to 12,000 rads of neutron and gamma rays, primarily on the right side of his body. Anything over 400 rads is considered lethal.

With the autopsy complete, the man in the suit now places the organs in wide-mouthed mayonnaise jars and prepares to send them to laboratories across the country.

Gunther von Hagens's first inkling that there might be a market for his plastinated creations beyond the needs of academia came in 1983. The Catholic Church, suddenly uncertain whether an eight-hundred-year-old miracle could still be trusted, contacted von Hagens with a proposal to use his technique to preserve the shriveled heel of Saint Hildegard. Although the holy relic was not, eventually, entrusted into his care, von Hagens was intrigued by the thought that there may be commercial possibilities for his work.

This idea was bolstered when, one night, he entered his lab to finish a few neglected tasks and found one of the building's janitors gawking at a group of plastinated limbs laid out on a table. Surprised and delighted at the layman's interest, von Hagens, now head of his own company, considered for the first time a public exhibition. In 1988, he mounted a small display of organs in a hall in Pforzheim, Germany, and after fourteen thousand people attended in a two-week period, he made plans for a much larger showing that would feature whole cadavers.

In 1995, *Body Worlds: An Exhibition of Real Human Bodies* opened at Juntendo University in Japan. Von Hagens's intention had been to host the show closer to home, but he had difficulty finding a space to exhibit his stable of cadavers for the general public. Continental museums were uncomfortable with the idea of corpses on display, and besides, it seemed likely that the show would only appeal to a small portion of the population, not the families that are such institutions' bread and butter.

But then 400,000 visitors attended the Japanese *Body Worlds* show during its two-month limited engagement. The show's run was extended and the people kept coming. It was a phenomenal success, bringing a total of 2.9 million attendees and staying open three years after its original closing date. In Von Hagens's words, "Everything changed for me after Japan." Suddenly museums in Germany, Austria, Switzerland, and the United Kingdom were clamoring for a *Body Worlds* of their own.

As the exhibits toured throughout Europe and the United States, public interest in the shows only seemed to grow. Von Hagens, with his black fedora and undeniable showman's charisma, became a celebrity, granting numerous interviews and appearing in a host of television segments featuring his plastinated creations. In 2002, his carnival-barker instincts stoked a fire of controversy when he, in perhaps another homage to *Dr. Nicolaes Tulp,* announced plans to perform the first public autopsy in Britain in over 170 years. Despite an outcry and concerns that the performance might be illegal, the event's tickets quickly sold out, and an audience of five hundred filled the gallery as von Hagens sawed through the skull of a seventy-two-year-old man, and many more watched the event's live broadcast on their televisions at home. It was then that von Hagens's nickname Dr. Death, already in use in his native Germany, gained international currency, putting him, perhaps unfairly, in the dubious ranks of other Dr. Deaths—Jack Kevorkian, Eric Pianka, Josef Mengele.

Interest in *Body Worlds* skyrocketed, and the original plastination lab in Germany was no longer capable of keeping up with demand. Von Hagens opened two more plastination centers, one in Kyrgyzstan and one in Dalian, China, locations chosen for having ready access to skilled, low-cost technicians.

It was at the Chinese plant that von Hagens encountered his first real problems. One of the factory managers, seeing an opportunity to capitalize on a hungry and extremely lucrative marketplace, defected from the *Body Worlds* company and opened up a rival plant in the same city. Unconcerned with the rigorous consent process that von Hagens insisted on utilizing to obtain bodies for the exhibits, the new plant instead purchased unclaimed corpses from the Chinese Ministry of Public Security, which, ominously, does not keep documents detailing the circumstances of the subjects' deaths, leading some to speculate that they may be those of executed prisoners. Von Hagens attempted to sue the new company, but the murky channels of Chinese intellectual property law rebuffed him at every turn. As the new factory began churning out cut-rate cadavers, rival exhibition companies, hungry for a share in *Body Worlds*' success and emboldened by von Hagens's legal difficulties, began to mount their own exhibits in England, Korea, and the United States.

The show I am attending in Albuquerque is one of the knock-offs. Created and promoted by the Atlanta-based Premier Exhibitions, *Bodies: The Exhibition* is, in many ways, a fun house mirror of von Hagens's *Body Worlds*. Where *Body Worlds* plays exclusively in high-profile museums in major cities throughout the world, *Bodies: The Exhibition* is more likely to exhibit in shopping malls, convention centers, casinos, and other "nontraditional" venues. Where *Body Worlds* is renowned for the professional quality of its displays—the angelic lighting, the pitch-perfect mood music, and the immaculately presented cadavers themselves—*Bodies: The Exhibition*, though it apes these trappings, is beset by the issues that come with its second-string venues: cracked floors, poor lighting, cavernous spaces partitioned off by temporary walls. But despite the shoddy settings of its exhibits, and the questionable origins of its cadavers, Premier Exhibitions recently posted a quarterly profit of $4.9 million.

The body with the football still commands my attention. It stands upon a wooden block on wheels. I am surprised at how small it is; even on its pedestal it is still shorter than I am, and the epicanthic fold of its eyelids is a disturbing indication of its Asian gray-market origin. A family is beside me, examining it, laughing in surprise at its nakedness, pointing at the shriveled penis that hangs between its fleshless legs. Embarrassed, I move to the second room, where an even more diminutive cadaver stands with a conductor's baton in its fingers, the muscles pulled away on much of its body to show the spaghetti-like strands of nervous system as they stretch across its chest, its legs, its arms, all the way to its fingers. In the third room wait the majority of the cadavers; these, too, are all short statured and possessed of epicanthic eyelids. In one corner, a cadaver prepares to serve a volleyball. In another, a woman is cut lengthwise into thirds, the portions of body standing upright, side by side. The centerpiece of the room is a man sliced thin as deli meat, each of the dozens of prosciutto sections of the body sandwiched between glass and suspended in a case.

In von Hagens's first exhibitions, the bodies had been displayed in a prosaic fashion: standing straight, arms at their sides, bare-muscled faces forward. Visitors complained that they seemed cold and frightening, somehow blind in their absent expressions—too much, in fact, like dead things. One of the hallmarks of the plastination process is that once a cadaver has been impregnated with the polymer, it can be held in virtually any position, and as *Body Worlds* exhibits opened in Europe, von Hagens positioned the cadavers into more dynamic poses: kicking a soccer ball, throwing a football, playing badminton. "I took the fear out and put the humor in," he explained, and for the most part, visitors responded favorably to the more whimsically posed corpses.

When the rival exhibitions began to appear, they mimicked these poses, but von Hagens upped the ante. Basketball and badminton now bored him, and he pushed further. Soon he was making the bodies dance in ways that his competition had difficulty keeping up with: cadavers as ballerinas, playing in poker games, hanging from gymnastic rings, contemplating chess with skull opened and brain exposed; a rider on flayed and rearing horseback; a body holding up its preserved skin like a cast-off bathrobe; a corpse lying on its side, belly sliced to show the eight-month fetus inside it; another in a sleigh pulled by four plastinated reindeer. For von Hagens, the poses became a trademark, a point of pride, a chance to express an artistry in his work. As he continued to push into the realm of taboo, however, he was met with increasing outrage. Most recently, the city government of Berlin has threatened to ban one of the shows that feature his latest tableau: two cadavers positioned to simulate sexual intercourse. Von Hagens shrugged his shoulders. "An anatomical exposition without publicity is like a theatre without a program," he said, and the crowds kept coming.

A week later, Doris, Cecil Kelley's wife, stands beside her seven-year-old daughter as his casket is lowered into the grave at the Santa Fe National Cemetery. No tears well in her eyes—all the crying had happened while she sat in his hospital room, her husband still alive behind a row of cement blocks and an oxygen tent. As she spoke to him, he groaned and heaved and struggled to tell her to take good care of their children. A few hours later, she watched as the doctors extracted samples from his still-living body, a syringe of watery red material that she later described as "mush." She was there when he lapsed into unconsciousness, and his breaths turned to croaks. And she cried when, at 3:15 a.m. on New Year's Day of 1958, his body finally succumbed to the death that had been inevitable since he peered into the viewing port of the plutonium separation tank and saw the blue light of a critical chain reaction.

But now it is done, she thinks; his body is at rest.

Turning from the prosciutto man, I see a small, dark doorway leading away from the room. There is a disclaimer beside it, warning that the hall beyond holds specimens of fetuses in various stages of development, all of which "perished in utero from complications during pregnancy." I go in.

Inside, the fetuses are not plastinated, but rather suspended in bottles of preservation fluid, lit from below and luminescent in the dim room. They range from a minimal speck (only a week of development) to a child brought nearly to term, its skin somehow turned translucent, its skeleton visible. A group of women is in the room with me; they coo as they examine a six-month-old fetus. "Look at the tiny fingernails!" one exclaims, in precisely the same tone I heard my mother use while admiring my newborn son.

This bothers me. Three years before, during hunting season in Chadron, Nebraska where we had come for an AmeriCorps position, my wife miscarried in her twelfth week of pregnancy. The fetus had already died at some unknown point beforehand; an unexpected stillness on the ultrasound monitor prompted the technician to speak her words in measured, careful tones. The doctor prescribed a pill, and that night in a wood-paneled motel room, Courtney curled up in pain and squeezed my hand tighter than she ever had before or would again until the birth of our son two years later.

The doctor had warned us about the tiny fingers, about the possibility that it might look like a miniature baby, but it was undifferentiated among the blood and tissues, and we couldn't even be sure it was the fetus itself until the doctor had confirmed it.

The next morning, while Courtney slept, I walked the dogs in the motel parking lot among the trailer beds holding deer carcasses that bled from the mouth and I cried. I cried for a possibility that had never come into existence, for a person I would never know.

I suddenly don't want to be in this dark room with its floating fetuses and cooing spectators.

"A wide-mouthed mayonnaise jar. They packed my father's brain in a wide-mouthed mayonnaise jar," Katie Kelley, Cecil's daughter, says to reporter Ellen Wellsome in 1994. She has only recently found out that the body buried in the Santa Fe National Cemetery was incomplete, and that many of her father's internal organs and tissues were sent across the country for examination in various laboratories. She is incensed. Her mother says she never gave consent for this dismemberment, and although the government says she did, there are no records to prove it.

If there is magic in von Hagens's process, it is in its ability to remove life, and identity, completely. Some have said that Dr. Death grants his subjects a kind of immortality, but that is certainly the wrong word. Removing the corpse's skin, pulling the water out, and replacing it with plastic, makes the corpse both generic and deader than dead. A dead body in its natural state is only dead by one narrow set of criteria: Immediately after human life ceases, the bacteria in the stomach begin to flourish and break out of their former containment, spreading throughout the body and breaking down the tissues, soon joined by outside microbes and insect larvae—a discolored, bloating explosion of life.

But plastination, which impregnates every cell of tissue with silicone rubber, arrests that process entirely for an indefinite time. The human body, fluid in its transformations throughout its growing life, can now be frozen into an effectively eternal state: transition, transformation, growth, death, and change, all banished.

Stripped of identity, sealed off from the natural processes, it becomes *hyper-mortal*. A state of complete and total death; *beyond* death. The ultimate objectification.

Outside the fetus room, I hurriedly make my way past the trisected woman, the volleyball player, the racks of individual parts (legs, arms, faces), and toward the exit. There is a cadaver between me and it, and although I want to leave, I can't help but stop for one last look.

The body is, like most of the others, held in an athletic position, this time as though about to spin a discus. Alarmingly, there are sutures in its flesh, screws set into its arms, steel mesh covering a hole in its skull, and various medical tools jutting out of it on every side. A nearby plaque states that this cadaver showcases the wide variety of treatments that modern medicine can provide for injury, but the overall effect is more like a voodoo doll than a surgical model.

On impulse, I bring myself close to the body, my eyes tracing over the musculature of its face. I want to know who he was, this unknown man who died an unknown death in a faraway country. I wonder if his body went unclaimed because he was homeless, or a prisoner, or just alone when he died, one of the millions who left their families behind in rural villages in order to seek out work in the new China's neon cities. I wonder about the pins and clamps and staples that pierce and grip his body—were any of them there prior to his trip through the Dalian plastination factory? Or was he just decorated in this way to give a paying audience something to look at?

There are no answers in his face, as impassive and anonymous as all the others, and there is no way to bring his identity back, no matter how closely I look. I feel disgusted with myself as I turn away from him.

I walk past the makeshift gift shop and a table where a lab-coated woman offers a plastinated arm for guests to touch, toward the doors out of the hall.

I don't know what I was looking for when I came here today. I do know as I walk out into the glare of the Albuquerque sunlight that I have gained nothing and resolved nothing, that if what brought me here was a desire to be closer to the father who disappeared twenty years ago or the child who never made it far enough to have a name, plastinated cadavers could never have helped with that. Loss is still loss, and the vague ache somewhere down below would have ached to this day no matter what I had found in the exhibition.

If there is a truth that these anonymous mannequins offer, it has little to do with the mysteries of what awaits us beyond the body and more to do with the vulnerability of our physical forms themselves. After death, our bodies will belong to something else, whether bacteria feeding on them in an orgy of decomposition or a mad German doctor using them to build an empire or a knock-off company from Atlanta that purchases corpses and doesn't care where they come from.

It's 1994 and Clarence Lushbaugh, the man in the protective suit who dissected Cecil Kelley's body in 1958, is giving a deposition in response to a lawsuit over his treatment of Kelley's remains. Katie Kelley, the man asking the questions says, is distraught that her father was buried incomplete. Doris Kelley says she never gave consent for the autopsy or the later use of his tissues. Who gave you permission to do so?

God gave me permission, Lushbaugh answers.

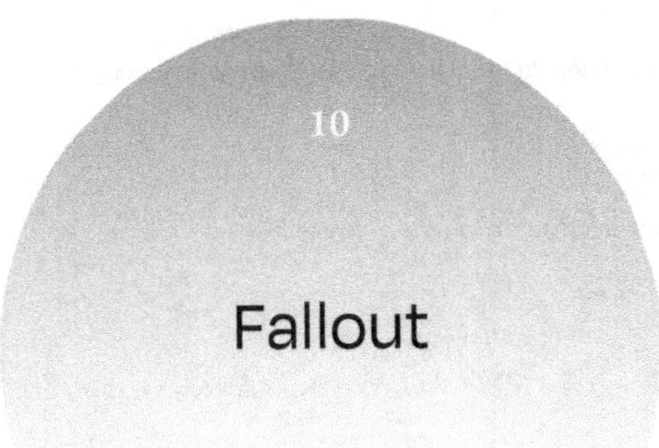

10
Fallout

Hey Bert . . .

LOOK OUT!

Oh my! DANGER!

Bert ducks and covers.

He's smart, but HE has his shelter on his back . . .

YOU must learn to find shelter.

You have learned how to take care of yourself in many ways—to cross streets safely.

And you know what to do in case of fire—b-u-t . . .

The atomic bomb is a NEW danger. It explodes with a flash brighter than any you've ever seen.

Things will be knocked down all over town.

And, as in a big wind, they are blown through the air. YOU must be ready to protect yourself.

So, like Bert, you DUCK to avoid the things flying through the air . . .

. . . and COVER to keep from getting cut or even badly burned.

Your city and its civil defense will try to warn you with a special alarm in time to go to a special shelter . . . Then . . .

you must go quickly and quietly to the special shelter as the block warden, your teacher or your parents tell you.

But sometimes—and this very important—the bomb might explode and the bright flash come . . . without any warning!

There is always SOMETHING to shelter you—indoors, a school desk, a chair, a table. Always duck away from windows and glass doors.

Outdoors, duck behind walls and trees. Even in a hollow in the ground. In a bus or auto, duck down behind or under the seats.

But remember . . . DO IT INSTANTLY . . . Don't stand and look. Duck and Cover!

—*Bert the Turtle Says Duck and Cover*, 1951

I recently met my mother for lunch in downtown Albuquerque, and I could still see the signs. Yellow rectangles, streaked with rust. A black circle behind three triangles pointing downward. FALLOUT SHELTER. Affixed and forgotten on the brick wall of one of the squat buildings that line Central Avenue.

During our meal, there were signs from her too. She got a faraway look in her eye and apologized in a way that she often does. "It wasn't fair," she said.

"We made it out all right," I answered.

"I just didn't know any better," she said.

When I was a child, my sister and I would hide in our bedroom while our parents argued. Door shut, we halfheartedly pretended to play while shouts erupted from the other room. As the argument reached its crescendo and my father's fist repeatedly struck a wall with explosive force and my mother's voice degenerated into wailing, my breath would stop and my sister would look at me with wide, terrified eyes.

"It's OK," I would say. "They'll stop soon." And inside my head, the echo *Stop soon. Please stop soon.*

Nope. Not fair. Not the worst, but certainly not fair.

Old shelter signs are everywhere in this town. In the back hall of a secondhand store that was once a JCPenney. In the basement of a college dormitory. On the street side of an abandoned high school. Places to hide, all over the city; reminders of an inherent, tenacious unfairness that once hung over the whole country, the whole world.

Nuclear attack: an ever-looming threat that never materialized.

I can't help but think of my own hiding spaces, and my father in the throes of his rage: a threat that materialized all too often.

Critical mass. Detonation. A swirl of anxiety, depression, and fear coalescing into a moment of destruction. Wild eyes, shouting voice, barely intelligible, and an outburst of violence. Heat, fire, a shock wave of force roiling across a landscape, walls falling, bodies incinerating, water boiling to steam.

Unstoppable. Unsurvivable. There is only one recourse.

To hide.

Danny Parker unlocks the metal double doors, revealing a short antechamber and stairs going down. Beside the doubles, there is a smaller door.

"What's this one for?" I ask, pointing to it.

"That goes to a decontamination area below. There's a shower there and a Geiger counter. You'd go in that one after the bomb had gone off. I'll show you."

He steps inside now. I follow, with my wife and children right behind. There's a huge, solid slab of metal with a handle nested into an alcove in the wall; another door, ready to swing out and seal the entrance completely behind a thousand pounds of steel. This one would have been used in the event of a nuclear attack. It has two purposes: protect the people inside from fallout and keep anyone outside from breaking in.

We are inside Abo Elementary School in Artesia, New Mexico, the only public school in the United States to be built entirely underground. Its primary function was to educate children, of course, but in the event of an emergency, it could house 2,100 people for approximately ninety days.

"Which twenty-one hundred people?" I ask.

"It would depend on who got here first," Danny says, and smiles.

I've come here to Artesia to explore this idea of hiding. I'm fascinated by it. There are many primal, instinctual responses, but hiding is the last one, the final attempt at survival. Whatever is threatening you is so awful, so strong, so destructive that neither fight nor flight is an option. All that's left is to go somewhere where it can't find you, to keep your breath quiet and your body still and hope and hope that it passes by.

I was a child well after the period of the Cold War when so many assumed that an attack was imminent, but we were still taught to hide when we needed to. When the sky would go dark in Houston and the emergency broadcasting system would flash across our television screen warning of tornadoes, my mother told us what to listen for. "The sound of a train," she said. "If you hear it, hide in the closet." But we never did. At least not for that.

It was their noises, the noises made by my parents, that we hid from. And as the sounds they made got worse, we became more and more still. Waiting for it to pass by.

As we walk through the empty hallways of the Abo school, my children and Danny's run like mad into darkened rooms and peek around corners. It isn't long before they've arranged an impromptu game of hide-and-seek.

I'm surprised at how much like a typical elementary school Abo actually is, at least once the lights are turned on. The rooms are carpeted and unassuming; some of the classrooms have the names of students still on the board, often with the date "May 22, 1995," Abo's last day as a functioning elementary school. I try to picture myself as a child going here, and decide that I would have probably enjoyed it. The grim reality behind its creation is easy to ignore.

It's only when Danny points out the various shelter features that the building's purpose becomes overt. The steel doors, of course, the decontamination shower, an air filtration system, a massive backup generator hulking in a room of its own. In the school's cafeteria, where the tables fold up into the walls for maximum space saving, a chin-up bar is incongruously mounted to a wall. "If people had been down here after an attack, they would have had their time scheduled for various activities, partly to keep them on a routine and to help keep them calm," Danny tells me. "One of them was exercise, so this bar was here for that purpose."

When we hid, we also tried to stay calm. The sounds outside our room grew louder and the shouting more incomprehensible, but we tried to play, tried to pretend it wasn't happening. Our games were quiet; our expressions stoic. When what you are afraid of is a part of your family, though, you hide from more than just the disasters and explosions. You learn to hide from their very possibility. Every conversation or interaction becomes a drill.

There is a tape I found recently. My sister made it with a Fisher-Price recorder—the kind with big colorful buttons and an indestructible plastic casing—when she was four years old. On the tape, it's my mother's birthday and my father is baking her a cake while she is at work. My sister, recording the moment, is talking to him while he mixes, asking endless questions in the way that four-year-olds often do. "Is there a cake yet?" she asks, over and over. "Is there a cake yet? Can I taste?"

At first, my father is patient and even sweet. "No, sugar, not yet. It's going to be a while."

But then, after several of her high-pitched, insistent questions, something happens. She asks again, "Can I taste?"—and it's like a switch is flipped.

My father is now yelling: "Goddamn it! I fucking said NO! Go to your room!" His voice is an eruption, a crack of thunder, and accompanied by a clatter as though he has slammed his hand down upon the countertop and disturbed the cooking implements there. Small wonder that she is now crying, wailing unintelligibly. "Jesus Christ, stop asking! I said NO! GO TO YOUR FUCKING ROOM!"

When I heard this tape, I remembered how often this sort of thing had happened. How we learned to guard ourselves against the outbursts that could come at any time. Leave Papa alone when he's working; go into the other room when you can; if you have to ask him a question, be meek and quiet. And always be ready.

Landra White was fifteen years old when her father built them a hiding place in their quiet residential neighborhood in Albuquerque. A corrugated Quonset hut, seventeen feet by twelve feet, was constructed above ground and lowered into an eleven-foot-deep pit.

Landra is now sixty-seven years old, a rounded, smiling woman with tousled hair and an infectious laugh. Her brother, Carl, who was ten years old when the shelter was constructed, has come with her to a sandwich shop to meet me and talk about the shelter.

"I wouldn't say that he was any more fearful than anyone else; he was just logical, you know," she says, speaking of her father, Chester White. "We knew that the nearby Manzano Mountains were just full of atom bombs. Actually, nuclear warheads. . . . We also knew that Albuquerque is a major crossroads for land transportation, so we knew that Albuquerque was a prime target, not for the first strike, but the second. They would want to knock out the transportation, especially for nuclear warheads."

Chester, a mechanical engineer by trade, put the finishing touches over the shelter—twelve-inch-thick concrete blocks around the perimeter of the hut, a five-inch-thick concrete slab to double as the family driveway—and then drove a front-end loader back and forth over the slab to compact the earth. A ventilation duct stuck out incongruously from the front yard. There were two entrances to the shelter: one a heavy steel door in the basement, the other a hatch leading out beside their driveway.

Abo and the White shelter were both built in 1962, a big year for fears of nuclear war. In late 1961, *Life* magazine had published a letter (with a faded mushroom cloud background) authored by President Kennedy, which read:

> The government is moving to improve the protection afforded you in your communities through civil defense. We have begun, and will be continuing throughout the next year and a half, a survey of all public buildings with fallout shelter potential, and the marking of those with adequate shelter for 50 persons or more. We are providing fallout shelter in new and in some existing federal buildings. We are stocking these shelters with one week's food and medical supplies and two weeks' water supply for the shelter occupants. In addition, I have recommended to the Congress the establishment of food reserves in centers around the country where they might be needed following an attack. Finally, we are developing improved warning systems which will make it possible to sound attack warning[s] on buzzers right in your homes and places of business. . . .
>
> I urge you to read and consider seriously the contents of this issue of LIFE. The security of our country and the peace of the world are the objectives of our policy. But in these dangerous days when both these objectives are threatened, we must prepare for all eventualities. The ability to survive coupled with the will to do so therefore are essential to our country.

A series of articles on surviving a nuclear attack followed: a column about community shelters; a rundown of tips on removing and disposing of fallout-contaminated clothing; a series of designs for backyard shelters that a family could install quickly and at low cost.

The possibility of nuclear attack was so horrific, so huge, and so powerful that hiding was the government's official recommendation.

Beneath President Kennedy's letter, a pull quote: "You could be among the 97% to survive if you follow the advice in these pages . . . How to build shelters . . . Where to hide in cities . . . What to do during an attack."

There are shelter designs, with artist renderings of the completed building, always with family members looking peaceful inside. The mother folds clothes, the daughter arranges her hair, the son reads a book, the father smokes a cigarette. While outside, somewhere nearby, the world is presumably burning.

There's even advice for those who have not had the foresight to build their own shelter. "Block up the basement windows with one foot of earth, and take shelter there under tables on which you have piled books and magazines for extra shielding." It seems like something I would have done as a child: Build a fort out of tables and books. Hide there and hope that you're safe.

In our room, the door was enough. Or perhaps it wasn't enough, but we knew that nothing would be enough if the time came. Piling books up against it, or chairs from the small table set against the wall, or pillows or stuffed animals—it wouldn't have even been worth the effort. There were no articles, no pamphlets, no manuals on how we could protect ourselves.

Hiding is about fear, and yet, the families pictured in the preparedness booklets are never shown as being afraid. They are always calm, detached, pursuing some semblance of their normal lives, their normal roles. When you hide, when you wait, you don't act fearful, really. You try to stay calm. Try to stay on top of things, pretend that what you're doing is normal, no matter what sounds are coming from outside.

The materials the Federal Civil Defense Administration (later the Office of Civil and Defense Mobilization) gave to children at the Abo school and across the country reinforce this controlled feeling of calm. Famously, children learned to "duck and cover" from Bert the Turtle, who demonstrated the technique in slideshows and animated films. Nuclear annihilation is represented by a monkey with a firecracker who sneaks up behind him. Other preparedness films showed families on picnics who react to the sight of a blinding flash by throwing a blanket over their heads. Booklets included plays children could perform in their classrooms or for their families: The characters excitedly shout, "We're going to have the best shelter in town!"

"I don't remember it being particularly sugarcoated, but I also don't remember being particularly nervous or upset about it," says Carl White after I asked him if he understood the purpose behind the family fallout shelter. "I mean, it was just sort of factual." He continues, "It's clear to me now that it was a fallout shelter, not a flash shelter, or a blast shelter. Just a fallout shelter."

"I mean, if Albuquerque was a strike zone, you know," adds Landra, "and we measure the blast from downtown to Hyder Park, and we're right in the middle of that, what are the chances that the shelter would even survive?"

As Chester himself wrote in "A Family Shelter Training Exercise," a document he compiled for the Office of Civil and Defense Mobilization, "This shelter was designed for protection against fallout contamination after a nuclear burst. Protection it might afford from a firestorm and nuclear blast was not the primary design intent."

But Chester adopted the idea that meticulous planning for survival was necessary even if the odds of actual survival were low. He arranged a series of meetings with the local branch of Civil Defense and laid out how the shelter would be stocked, what the day-to-day routine of life inside would be like, and what foodstuffs would go into fourteen days' worth of meals.

One day, toward the end of the winter of 1994, after the years of drills, the ducking and covering in our room only to emerge into the safety of the world we knew, there was finally an explosion.

My mother, always trying to understand him, would later offer a number of theories about what had been wrong with my father that day: He had been drinking, he was popping pills, the migraine medicine that he injected had caused a reaction. Sometimes her theories expand to include outlandish possibilities like crack or other drugs. Maybe she's right. But somehow, however he got there: critical mass.

My mother was on the ground. He was kicking her. She cried out in pain, a terrible animal sound. He ranted and frothed. There was broken crockery. A knife on the ground.

I pushed him off of her, against the stove. I punched him in the forehead, and he looked at me for a moment like he was going to kill me, but then turned away. I backed up to where my mother had been, but she was gone with my sister into the other room. I glared at him and picked up a glass from a nearby table with my left hand, because my right hurt.

Again, he looked at me, but his expression wasn't angry; it was tired. I shouted something and threw the glass at him, but it missed. The dog howled.

I backed into the other room. He followed. I went to the door. He followed, but instead of pursuing me, he sat in his recliner, *his* recliner, the one place in the living room that was fully, unquestionably his. Some part of him had risen up to protect us, perhaps; the rage was confronted by the reality of what he had done, and he collapsed into his chair, unable to move further. And the footrest extended with its customary *sproing* and he turned his eyes to the ceiling.

And we ran, and found shelter.

In the Abo school, we follow the hallways around, flicking on the lights as we go. By now, it seems utterly benign, an elementary school that happens to be underground. But then two things happen.

First, we come to a corner room with a low ceiling. There are shelves against the wall, but otherwise it is unremarkable. "If there'd been an emergency, they would have needed a place to store the bodies," Danny says. "This room was designated for the morgue."

It's chilling to look at, even if it is outwardly unremarkable. The fact of its existence is utilitarian: During the school year it would be used to hold books and other equipment; after an attack it would be used to hold bodies.

On the back wall, someone has taped up a drawing of Jesus in colored pencil.

We walk on, looking into the other classrooms. On the floor in one of them, there's a card, a little larger than a business card. I pick it up and read it.

> ***WARNING**WARNING**WARNING***
>
> Use only in correct caliber as inscribed on the barrel. The gun should never be pointed or fired directly at a person or animal because of possible injury. . . . For use in 9 mm long barrel only.

"Danny?" I ask, holding it up in front of me. "What is this?"

"It's instructions from a container of blank rounds," he says. "The building is sometimes used by the nearby Federal Law Enforcement Training Center for school shooter exercises." On the classroom's blackboard there are diagrams of the hallways showing the best locations for officers to position themselves. A circle represents an armed invader. From one type of disaster to another.

After the explosion, after we went to the police station and then the hospital (where we found out that my right hand was broken), we hid at a hotel near the freeway.

In our hiding place, at the hotel, we waited. Daytime television and trips to the ice machine. If we talked, I don't remember what it was about. I had school every day; I showed my friends my broken hand with the excuse that I had fallen off a bicycle. We worried about what might be happening at our house. Should we feed the dog? Should we get our stuff? We would go to the dollar theater and eat at the nearby Chili's and pass the time. Quiet, boring. Simply a matter of waiting. One day I fed a dollar into the soda machine and it spat out not only my soda but also quarter after quarter until there was a pile in my hands, more than I could hold, and then it spilled onto the floor. Ten dollars in all. And that's all there was.

After a few days, my mother called him from the hotel, and I could hear him crying on the other end. "Please come back," he said, his voice tinny on the receiver. "I can't live without you . . ."

He couldn't live without us. He was in danger, and we knew it. But he couldn't come with us, not now, because the danger we all faced, including him, was the danger from himself. He had exploded, he had attacked. And now we needed protection.

I know what it's like. The voices of our parents take up residence in our heads. Not only do I still hear him, but sometimes I feel him. The anger welling up, closer and closer to a breaking point, propelled by fear and anxiety. Not wanting to lose something precious as adrenaline floods the system, made worse with alcohol. I know what he felt like.

"I said, 'I want a divorce,'" my mother told me. She said it to him in the kitchen on the day of his attack, and then he snapped and turned on her like a savage animal, rage propelled by fear of abandonment. A desperate, irrational act. I know it. I've punched holes in walls, and sometimes turned my hands against myself.

So far, I stop. Usually, so did he. But that day, he couldn't. And we had to run from him and hide. He was hurt too, but he couldn't come with us. Not that day. Nor the day after that. Not for weeks. He was left out there, in our suddenly quiet house, in the world that he had made, while we hid from it, and from him. We had to keep our shelter closed against him. He couldn't come in.

One night, shortly before her family went into the shelter for a week-long drill—proposed by Civil Defense and publicized by newspapers and radio stations—Landra White lay in her bedroom, listening to the murmur of voices from the kitchen down the hall. Her parents were discussing their shelter with a man from CD. Suddenly, the man said something that made her eyes widen.

"I remember hearing them say something like, 'What are you going to do if people come and want to get in?' and then Dad said, 'We'll have the guns in the foyer.'"

When you're hiding, there are rules. When you are reduced to pure, primal survival, you can't let the outsiders in.

When Landra and her family entered the fallout shelter for the exercise, there was no question of it being anything other than a drill. Newspaper reporters interviewed them as they made ready to descend, cameramen took their pictures, and radio stations held remote broadcasts from the site.

Landra's job was to get fresh milk from the refrigerator; two of her brothers gathered bread and fresh vegetables. They went down the ladder and the hatch was closed and locked by Colonel Hancock of the Office of Civil and Defense Mobilization, who retained the key.

"It was boring," Landra says.

"It got long," adds Carl, "especially since we were all so close. Luckily, that's where having dark was a benefit. You could get on your cot and sort of be alone."

I wonder what would have happened to my family in a fallout shelter. Trapped in a space smaller than our living room, waiting two weeks for the radiation levels to fall. My father did not like to be trapped. He always sought escape from the noise of children, the demands of his marriage. What would rage have done to him down there? What would it have done to us?

Fortunately, there were no nuclear attacks, no fallout for people like the Whites or the children at Abo school to seek shelter from. In the decades since *Life* magazine spurred the boom in their creation, the shelters have almost all been abandoned. No longer stocked with food and water. No longer taken seriously. Some have been forgotten, some have been repurposed. In the public mind, they have become kitsch, a relic of a foreign age.

The White family's shelter is now used as an exercise room by the renters who live in their former home. Abo functioned as a school until 1995, when it needed renovations; an underground school is difficult and costly to update. Now it is used for storage and federal exercises like the school shooting training that had left the blanks behind. Danny Parker hopes that someday it will be a museum. Most of the others have succumbed to similar fates: A major bunker in Boise, Idaho, once capable of holding a thousand people for weeks after a detonation, has become a studio for music room rentals. While clearing ground for a shopping mall in San Jose, California, the crew found a network of underground tunnels and rooms filled with water. It was a shelter from the '60s, but they had no idea who built it. In a Watkins Glen, New York, middle school, a librarian opened a disused half door in the corner of a basement and found three interconnected shelter rooms, still stocked from the '60s, old boxes covered in dust. The shelter was not listed on any documents.

We no longer fear nuclear attack like we once did, but the bombs are still there—7,700 in the United States as of 2013, 8,500 in Russia, a few hundred in France and China, Pakistan and India. Seventeen thousand total worldwide, and just as destructive and terrifying as ever. Our leaders say they are committed to not using them; nonproliferation treaties have replaced the government recommendation to hide in holes in the ground, and slowly, they are being dismantled. Hopefully, that is enough.

Instead of the worldwide doom once predicted, we are left with the small disasters of our everyday lives. Explosions and fallout that roil through families like mine. Fearful hiding and deadly blasts, the contamination that was here before and continues to exist beyond the crisis.

Since the term was coined in 1949, "fallout" has taken on meanings beyond the particles of radioactive dust that rain from the sky after a nuclear explosion. These days, "fallout" has come to mean any lingering, adverse effect that results from a negative situation.

For me, the danger has also faded, but never really disappeared. My home, the rooms where we hid from my angry father, was devastated by a hurricane, remodeled into something unrecognizable, and then rented out. The hotel by the highway is still there, but the Chili's and the dollar theater are both gone. My father is dead, but an echo of his rage and fear lurks somewhere inside my mind, and in the mind of my sister, who once hid with me. Sometimes it threatens to spill out and hurt the people we care about.

I have two children now. They make me angry sometimes, as does my wife. The anger rises up into levels that make me afraid. I remember my father's eyes and I worry that my own flash in the same way. When it happens now, I go into another room, remove myself from the conflict, focus on my breathing, hide for just a moment. Take shelter until the danger is past.

"It wasn't fair," my mother repeats. "He loved you, you know. He just didn't know how to control himself."

I try to keep it in check. I see a therapist and I take medication. My children do not hide in their room, even when my wife and I argue. Slowly, I tell myself, I am dismantling those old bombs. And hopefully, that is enough.

11

Plowshares

And he shall judge among the nations, and shall rebuke many people; and they shall beat their swords into plowshares, and their spears into pruning hooks; nation shall not lift up sword against nation, neither shall they learn war anymore.

—Isaiah 2:4

It's a late-winter day in Albuquerque, and a wind from the north has kicked up clouds of dust and mixed it with pollen from juniper trees that have been tricked into an early fructification by a warm snap. The whole city seems to be having an allergy attack, and even the crisp sunshine doesn't alleviate the feeling of unease.

As for me? Well, my hands are shaking.

A thousand feet below the granite sands of southeastern New Mexico, there is a great cave. Unlike the nearby Carlsbad Caverns, this space—170 feet wide and 90 feet high—was human-made. It is the result of Project Gnome, the first nuclear detonation in Project Plowshare, an attempt to find a peaceful use for the destructive energy of an atomic bomb. The scientists hoped that detonating a three-kiloton bomb underground would produce enough intense heat to manufacture steam for the purpose of generating electricity.

Plowshare's goals were straightforward and, I think, admirable, even if they ultimately turned out to be misguided. A fission detonation releases an incredible amount of energy, and so far, humanity had only managed to use that energy for destructive purposes, for war. Surely, there was a way mankind could channel it into something constructive.

I'm reading the past like tea leaves, like Rorschach ink blots. These chapters have veered off course into a dark riddle at the heart of my family. But still, I follow the threads of nuclear history. Even though I've lost my way, I want meaning from it, I want my own life reflected back at me. I'm desperate, though. A nervous energy courses through me as I type.

On December 10, 1961, the Gnome bomb was lowered down a long vertical shaft deep into the darkness of an ancient salt formation, then detonated. The surface of the ground lifted six and a half feet before collapsing down to its normal level. As scientists cheered, a pipeline pumped water into the cavity below, where it mixed with superheated molten salt and became steam.

But, according to the AEC's report, "At approximately seven minutes after zero time, a gray smoke, steam, and associated radioactivity surged from the shaft opening. By eleven minutes following the explosion, copious quantities of steam issued from both shaft and ventilation lines. A large flow continued for about thirty minutes before gradually decreasing. A small flow was still detected through the following day."

Somehow, the steam managed to travel back up the bomb's shaft (which did not self-seal as had been expected), pushing its way through the space between rubble, and then finally broke through to the surface.

Despite this unexpected leak, the AEC claimed that it was happy with the results.

Six months after the Gnome shot, the AEC deemed that the cavity would now be safe for human entry. Scientists drilled a new shaft into the space and opened it up. Inside, the salt—melted and displaced by the heat from the explosion—had cooled into staggering, colorful formations. Stalactites of violet and red dripped from the ceiling and swirls of golden amber striped across the walls of the cave.

The exploration team gazed up in wonder even as they wiped the sweat from their foreheads: It was still 140 degrees inside the cavity.

It's an anxiety attack. Heart rate elevates, hands begin to shake, thoughts are wild and careening from worry to worry, shame to anger, anger to fear, fear to guilt, guilt back to anger. I've had them many times, but that's not comforting. Still, knowing what's happening could at least save me some money; my trip to the hospital from an imagined heart attack recently cost me a $5,000 blemish on my credit history to find out that it was all in my mind.

I know why this one has been triggered. These aren't pleasant subjects. I feel like I'm betraying my family. The other night, I asked my mother to tell me about her experience with my father's rage throughout their marriage. She cried. Is it fair to ask her to relive these things? For what? For a book? It seems cheap. Besides, it's not good enough. And no one will want to publish it, much less read it, anyway. I place my hands on the table and try to focus on my breath.

"There were conditions," my mother said, when I asked her about the reconciliation. "He had to go into counseling. He had to go into AA. I picked him up and took him to court because he didn't have anything. The Cadillac he drove was on empty. And of course, he was safe as a lamb then."

In the courtroom, he kept his eyes down, his body collapsed. Charges were dropped on the condition that he sought help. "I told them that he had never hit me before, but that wasn't true. He'd given me a black eye before you were born. And then he'd hit me on the beach in front of our friends."

So, we moved back in. I had a cast on and he told me that he was proud of me for forcing him off of my mother. I didn't know what to say.

The AEC had been pleased with the Gnome shot at the time, but as the years went by, other scientists raised concerns. When called to testify on the effects of the detonation before Congress, thyroid expert Dr. Eric Reiss stated that Gnome had delivered enough fallout to nearby Carlsbad to expose children to "7 to 55 rads" of radiation. Doctors in the town reported an increase in the rates of congenital heart disease and other birth defects soon after.

Now the metaphor has risen above the facts. There were no nukes in my life in Seabrook, Texas, and our lives were not informed by them, except that they had brought my parents together geographically. Their influence, to the extent that it existed, was in the background.

We came back to live with him, but we were afraid. Children in Carlsbad developed congenital heart defects. Iodine-131, a radioactive isotope known to cause thyroid diseases, floated through the air, sending a long arm of fallout northeast through the United States. I asked my mother too many questions and she broke down in tears. The police came to our house again and found me huddled on the floor.

At this point, I can't extricate the threads. At this moment, they're all one and the same.

Project Sedan left a huge hole in the Nevada desert on July 6, 1962. The goal was two-fold: Attempt to place an explosive device so that (a) it removed the maximum amount of earth from the area and (b) released the minimum amount of radiation. If the test was successful, it would open a whole new world of uses for nuclear explosives, from carving a path for an interstate through mountainous terrain to creating artificial harbors in rocky coastlines, to tunneling underground connections between aquifers. The project's scientists determined that placing the device 650 feet below the surface would allow a sufficiently large crater while blocking the majority of fallout from entering the atmosphere.

The device, a 104-kiloton thermonuclear bomb, was put in place and detonated. The desert surface rumbled 300 feet into the air before exploding 11 million tons of soil outward in great tentacled billows, obscuring a five-mile diameter area before settling. The hole it left behind was 300 feet deep and 1,300 feet wide, the largest human-made crater in the United States.

But there was no doubt that a fusion bomb could make a big hole. The question had always been if it could do so without the release of a harmful amount of radiation. Once again, government sources at the time stated that the answer was "yes." An AEC-produced film on the Sedan shot touts the project as an unambiguous success.

But as the years went by, findings from the civilian press and the scientific community began to tell a different story. According to Dr. Edward Martell, who had monitored fallout for the government during that time, tests like Sedan were responsible for elevated levels of Iodine-131. The US Department of Health and Human Services lists Sedan as responsible for 7 percent of all fallout exposure to the civilian population in the United States, and in the downwind town of Pleasant Grove, Utah—where the fallout cloud drifted and eventually settled after making its way through Nevada—leukemia rates soared to over ten times the national average during the decade after the test.

Again, I can't pull this away from myself. The residual effects, falling from the air, seeping into the groundwater, ingested by cows and absorbed by crops, eaten by children, lodging in their bones and slowly killing them.

I'm lost at this point. My mind immediately returns to the explosions in my family. I can't help it. I've trained myself.

But is it wrong to impose a metaphoric interpretation? I don't even know; I can't extricate myself. These things happened, these things are happening, and I see myself in them.

My anger comes at a moment's notice, a sudden surge in adrenaline triggered by anxiety, by fear, by deep-seated feelings of self-hatred. A minor trigger in the outside world: I sit, untalked to and untalking at a party; I struggle to complete a story, an essay; my wife comments on something and I take it as a criticism; a mentor makes an offhand comment that sinks into my stomach like a fist. I find any stupid reason to be upset with myself. A pit opens up and a blackness lurks at its bottom, then creeps outward, festers, exacerbated by alcohol or sleep deprivation or what have you. Then it bursts for no good reason.

A flushing madness; the heart begins to thud, the breathing becomes shallow, the brain begins to scream. *It's over, they know how stupid you are, they will leave you, you will have nobody left. You don't deserve this. You need to escape. You need to die.*

I've put holes through walls with my fist, I've strung nooses from patio rafters, I've broken mirrors. One night, the night I came closest to actually killing myself, a police officer stayed outside my house for four hours while my wife tried to convince him to leave. She knew there was no way I'd come back if he was there. Finally, I promised him over the phone that I would check into the university mental health center if he would just go. He did. And I did.

But here's the thing: I don't necessarily seem that bad off. I can maintain. The very act of going to the clinic re-centered me, and by the time the doctor, thin and bald with thick glasses, saw me, I was pulling it off. He released me that night with a prescription for Xanax.

He shouldn't have. I was back a week later. This time, he looked at me and didn't talk. Then, with a sigh he said, "Mr. Bannerman, I don't quite know what to do with you. You shouldn't be reacting this way."

Of course not. That's why I was there. He sent me home again.

Here is what helps me: breathing in for four counts, breathing out for five; letting my thoughts drift through my mind, visualizing them floating through an open door and out an open window without finding purchase; therapy, frank discussion of the incidents with a disinterested third party. And medication.

"He was definitely self-medicating," my mother explained. "We found so many pills after he died. I don't even know what half of them were. He had two doctors, which is classic for somebody addicted to pills. He was drinking a half-bottle of NyQuil to try and go to sleep at night."

My mother has other theories about his self-medication. She wonders openly if he wasn't actually going to Alcoholics Anonymous but rather Narcotics Anonymous. "Alcoholism is the socially acceptable addiction," she said. "But he never really seemed to drink that much. And I know he had co-workers who smoked crack and other things. I just don't know what was going on. There were all these lighters in his office. And tire gauges. A friend of mine told me that people use tire gauges for smoking crack. I just don't know."

I looked on the Internet for info about tire gauges used as crack pipes. It turns out that it's a real phenomenon. There are even YouTube videos giving instructions on how to do it. But I have no idea if my father smoked crack, and neither does my mother. It's all theories, trying to reconstruct a mystery. Probably she will never know what was going on with him, and neither will I. But it seems clear that he was in pain, and that he had been trying for a long time to stop the pain, one way or another. I know what it's like to be in the grip of the kind of intense anger that he felt, how scary it is. The remorse and self-accusation that follows. How you wonder if you will be able to get it back under control, how you wonder what may happen next time, if you'll go too far.

"One day," she said. "He fell on his knees in the bedroom, crying his eyes out. He was saying, 'I tried to stop, but I couldn't. I couldn't stop.' I thought maybe he meant the alcohol, but now I don't know."

"What was it like for you?" I asked. "Moving back in. Were you afraid?"

She looked me in the eyes. "I put a fillet knife under our mattress. I was damn sure it wasn't ever going to happen again."

There was a hard hat that hung in my grandfather's garage. White beneath a spotting of dirt and dust, its ribbed sides spray-painted with stenciled images. Of course, I would wear it when I was a kid—it was by far the best headgear for a dragon-fighting knight or a cyborg soldier or whatever I was pretending to be that day. But even when I wasn't playing, I would sometimes hold it in my hands, running my fingers over its fiberglass curves, wondering about the simple black images on its sides.

The first was an aardvark, crouching low. The second, a duck, or perhaps a goose. The third an ostrich. The fourth, a martini glass. The fifth, a corkscrew. Aardvark, duck, ostrich, martini, corkscrew. Like the pantheon of a lost and idiosyncratic civilization, come down through time to rest on the shores of the present. Pictographs. Hieroglyphics.

"Bombs," my grandfather answered when I asked. "They were bombs we tested. Each one had a code name. Aardvark, Cormorant, Moa, Daquiri, Bordeaux. I wore that helmet for all of them."

I wanted to know more.

"Can't tell you," he answered with a tight-lipped grin. "Top secret."

In the poster-sized photograph in my grandmother's living room, a team of men, including my grandfather, are lowering a 33-kiloton bomb into a narrow shaft in the earth. The shaft extends 6,689 feet underground. It's a bright day in the arid hills of western Colorado in 1973, and the explosive device is one of three that will be detonated side by side. Like other Plowshare tests, the aim is to determine how useful a fission bomb could be for guiding the flow of natural gas and making it easier to collect, a sort of nuclear fracking.

It must have been thrilling. My grandfather, the son of a rail-riding transient who spent his childhood in the industrial sections of Seattle and Los Angeles, was now an integral part of a cutting-edge government project. One that would have allowed the tremendous science and research being performed as part of the United States' nuclear defense to be channeled into constructive uses. Of course he must have been excited as the countdown began, happy when the earth buckled beneath their feet, ecstatic when the gas began to course through the newly created chimneys at more than 40 percent in excess of their projections.

But then the flow slowed, and stopped. It seemed as though the chimneys were blocked with rubble. Hydraulic pumping managed to free up a little more, but hardly the amounts that they had been hoping for. What was worse, when the gas was tested, they found it was far too radioactive for commercial use. The scientists declared the test a failure, sealed the shafts, pumped the contaminated water into an underground well for long-term storage, and, after this final straw—combined with the increased public antinuclear sentiment of the mid-1970s—abandoned Project Plowshare.

The medication seems to help me more than any other approach. And as a stalwart believer in free will who fears that there is no such thing, I hate to admit that. But the brain is a chemical machine and my experiences are a direct result of my brain's interpretation of those chemicals, so I've made peace with the fact that a delicately applied outside chemical may help in the long run.

Two pink pills at night, every night.

At first, I shook even more than usual. There was a strange energy associated with the onset of the drug, and racing thoughts and shaking hands went with it. But now it's settled in me. The anxiety attacks last less time, overall. The depression passes quickly. Suicidal ideation usually goes by like a momentary daydream.

But it's not a permanent solution. These responses live deep inside me; they are a part of who I am, of my legacy. There is no magic bullet here, just management and hope. Day by day.

Now, for instance, the energy is bubbling up. My brain reads whatever is happening out in the world—in this case, the fact that I've made my mother cry when she talked about her history with my father—as a threat, but it doesn't know what to do with it. The amygdala is triggered, the impulses are traveling toward the frontal lobe. Adrenaline courses into my bloodstream, causing the heart to race, the breathing to become rapid and shallow.

But there's a difference: The chemical citalopram is also in my blood, insinuating itself between neurons, inhibiting the action of serotonin, which, through reasons that scientists do not entirely understand, allows the signals to my frontal lobes to be transmitted more effectively. There is now a slightly better chance that my rational brain will kick in before the tyranny of the amygdala enters full swing.

In other words, the problem, the propensity to anger, rage, anxiety, is still there. The citalopram simply gives a boost to the rational part of the brain in the hope that that will be enough to make a difference. Usually, it is.

For my father, it seemed that no matter what he did, he was stuck with his anger. And, I realize, so am I. Emotional conditioning is pernicious.

It's a legacy, one that extends back in my family line at least to my grandmother, probably further. How can you change who you are? You just live with it.

The worst part is knowing that, deep down, no matter how many breathing techniques you employ, no matter what medication you are on, it still could come erupting back. And that it may just be a matter of time.

For my father, the time did not come again. He died, in bed, on a Friday morning at the age of forty-three, only three months after the January incident. I don't know why this happened. Again, my mother theorizes that there may have been drugs involved, or that he was going through a withdrawal. I only know for sure that he was not very healthy, that he didn't take care of himself. His skin was yellow, his eyes sunken. Muscle had turned to flab and he seemed small. But I also know that he acted fine the night before. I came in from a play rehearsal and we watched an episode of *The Simpsons* together. He had recorded it because we both loved it and he wanted to see it with me.

And the next morning, he was gone. There was no autopsy, no explanation. It happened and it happened and I don't know why.

I'm forty-eight as I write this. Five years older than him.

I guess I've made it, but for how long?

After the Plowshare program ended, the United States gave up on finding peacetime applications for nuclear explosives. It was too dangerous and too many people raised their voices against it.

But the United States and other countries continued to make bombs and build up great stockpiles. Cynically, I agree with Dorothy Vanderford—I can't help but think that there will eventually come a day when they are used again for warfare, but for the time being, at least, it seems unlikely. There is enough concern in the world to keep it at bay, at least for a while.

Still, maintenance and manufacture continue to create dangerous waste. As has been the case all along, the question of how to keep civilians from being exposed to it remains an enigma.

The current solution to the waste problem is burial. The Waste Isolation Pilot Plant in southeastern New Mexico, mere miles away from the Project Gnome site, is an underground facility designed to store radioactive waste from weapons manufacture in a salt basin for the next ten thousand years. After ten thousand years? Who knows?

But even as I research it for this chapter, I find old news from WIPP. In October of 2016, a boulder of salt crashed down from the supposedly stable ceiling of the facility, crushing a truck deep in the plant's inner recesses. The truck caught fire, damaging portions of the facility and prompting worker evacuation from the site. No radioactive materials were compromised, they said at the time. But days later, an alarm began blaring in the tunnels, indicating that radioactive particles were present in the air at unsafe levels.

My heart has slowed down again, and my hands have stopped shaking. I spend a few moments focused on my breathing, letting the frantic thoughts unravel as they will, and now I open my eyes. I feel better, even if there's still a roaring in my ears, even if I know I'll have to deal with these feelings again and again for the rest of my life. At least they're gone for the moment. And at least I'll have some ability to deal with them when they come back.

"You're better with it than your father was," my mother said. "He needed therapy from when he was young, but we couldn't afford it. It's better now. I'm glad you've sought help."

I think she's right, but "better" is frustratingly subjective. How much risk is "OK"? How much of this danger should I feel comfortable passing down to my children?

Someday WIPP will be sealed, a tomb for a dark chapter of our history, perhaps the first of many. Theoretically, the surface will be safe. But ten thousand years is a long time, and the engineers worry about what obligation we have to the people of the future. How do we keep them away from the site? How can we tell them how dangerous it is? Especially since we ourselves do not have solutions for the problems contained inside?

There are plans to post a warning when the site is sealed, a warning to tell the people of the future that the problem of radiation-contaminated waste is still with them, deep beneath the earth.

One version of the warning is a plaque with these words upon it:

> This place is not a place of honor . . . no highly esteemed deed is commemorated here . . . nothing valued is here.
> What is here is dangerous and repulsive to us. This message is a warning about danger.
> The danger is in a particular location . . . it increases towards a center . . . the center of danger is here . . . of a particular size and shape, and below us.
> The danger is still present, in your time, as it was in ours.
> The danger is to the body, and it can kill.
> The form of the danger is an emanation of energy.

The danger is unleashed only if you substantially disturb this place physically. This place is best shunned and left uninhabited.

It doesn't seem like enough. Rereading it, I realize it's not even a warning. It's an apology. An apology for a legacy we can't control or eliminate.

EPILOGUE

Dr. Death arrived at the house at nine in the morning on his e-bike. He was wearing a purple shirt, khaki pants, and Birkenstocks. He was affable and slight, with a calm affect that was by no means morbid, and introduced himself with a firm handshake. One of us, probably Bruce, showed him the way to Grandma's room.

"Bernice!" he said, at an elevated volume. My grandmother lay in her bed, shrouded by the sheets. Her arms were exposed, and on her left she wore a bandage from wrist to elbow, another wound from tearing her too-fragile skin.

"Who's that?" she answered weakly.

"It's Dr. Fielder!" he said. "Do you remember what day it is?"

We stood beside her bed, my wife, my uncle, my mother, and me. Courtney and I had driven up from Albuquerque the night before and slept on the flat roof beneath semi-clouded New Mexico stars. My mother arrived in the morning, pulling her car up the steep gravel driveway only a few minutes before the doctor arrived.

"Well," Grandma answered. "Let's see . . ." She trailed off.

Truth be told, she was dying already and had been for weeks, if not months. During the COVID years, she had declined rapidly, her form growing thin and frail, her sight and hearing receding until all she could see were patches of light in the darkness and she could not hear our answers when she spoke to us on the phone. Over the last few weeks, she had begun to hallucinate, to see people who were not there. The night before, she described one to us.

"A woman with . . . with something she's been weaving. A blanket, I think. She's waving . . ."

Bruce—my uncle, her son—said that this had been going on for the last month. "It's rough. She'll suddenly shout from the living room. Say that she's ready to go home. 'But you are home,' I'll tell her, and she'll answer, 'It doesn't feel like home.' And in the middle of the night, she'll call out that there's someone at the foot of the bed. Sometimes she says it's Dan."

Dan was her husband, dead for thirty years.

The end of everything has already begun. In fact, if you'll bear with me, the beginning of the end of everything began at the beginning. From the moment of creation, entropy was here as well.

Entropy itself is not the end, but a sort of road that takes us there. Put simply, entropy is the transition from organization to disorganization, and necessary for the existence of all that we know. An organized system has fewer potential combinations. A disorganized system has more. And as time progresses, everything in the universe will move toward the maximum number of potential combinations. Gas will diffuse. Radioactive particles will escape from their host atoms. Humans will die and decay. Galaxies expand and separate. The universe itself spread thin.

"I'm going to need you to sit up!" Dr. Fielder said, still speaking loudly against the decay of her hearing.

"OK," she answered, and she moved her arms. My mother set up some pillows behind her and then she and my uncle helped her body to a sitting position.

"It's a special day!" Dr. Fielder said. "Do you remember what day it is?"

“One day . . .” she murmured. “One day out of a thousand.”

“Yes, but what did we talk about last week?” he asked.

“Today . . . today I’m going to just . . . disappear.”

“Yes, but I need you to be more specific than that,” he said. “Can you tell me, exactly, what you want to happen today?”

“I want . . . I’m ready . . . to die,” she said.

“And it’s your wish to die today?” he asked.

“Yes,” she said, firmly, even through the quaver of her ninety-seven-year-old voice.

The bomb generation left their mark upon us. They made us. And now we struggle with what they’ve made. All generations find themselves here, created by those who came before, making those who come after, struggling with the legacy we inherit, trying to shape the one we will give to our children. But the atomic generation, the way they shaped the world, was profound: the fall of Nazism and communism, the rise of American power, and the threat of global catastrophe in a form far quicker and more effective than any that ever came before.

What do we do with this? I want to ask them, as a whole. Do we have to keep it? Can we get rid of it somehow? Would it help?

Atomic stockpiles languish or grow, warheads are constructed or dismantled, but our knowledge and intent remain, seemingly as long lasting as the fissile material itself. As long as there is a bomb, there is a possibility of using it. So we look at this world they left us and we wonder, what do we do? Can we stave off disaster forever?

Good news. Nothing is forever.

In four and a half trillion years, the last atom of uranium will decay into lead. Problem solved.

Of course, we will be long gone by then, either through our destruction or an evolution into another form alien to us. If we can just hold out a little longer.

If, through some miracle, we do make it to four and a half trillion, then we won't have to worry about it anymore, but that's no mean feat. Life itself, at least on our planet, has only existed for three and a half billion years. But if one of us can get there, they can watch as the last atom of uranium sheds its final alpha particle and lapses into something inert, something quiet, something, dare I say, harmless.

Physician-assisted death has been legal in New Mexico since 2021, and in the three years since, I was surprised that Grandma had not chosen to pursue it. One of her primary pleasures as she got older was reading, and the last few years had stripped that away. By 2020, she was barely able to walk. By 2023, she could just manage to be helped from her bed to the easy chair on the porch to the dining table and back again. By 2024, she was falling regularly and Bruce sometimes had to call the fire department to help her get back up.

"OK, we're going to need to get her propped up again," Dr. Fielder said. "Can you help her with that?"

My mother and my wife began setting up pillows, then took my grandmother's arms and pulled her to a more upright position.

"And, Bernice, what we're going to do is give you a few minutes now to visit with your family while I go into the kitchen and get the medicine."

"OK," she answered, weaker than before.

The medicine had arrived the day before in an oval-shaped metal box, secured by combination lock. Inside was . . . who knows? A cocktail of substances compounded by a pharmacy in Albuquerque was then delivered by courier to a hilltop home on the outskirts of Santa Fe. Phenobarbital, perhaps, and morphine, maybe, to send her to sleep. And then rocuronium and propofol to relax the muscles of the body to the point where the heart stops.

"So I will prepare the medicines," Dr. Fielder continued, "and I'm going to come back with the medicines and with some raspberry sorbet."

"Oh, all right!" my mother said.

"I will give you a few teaspoons of the raspberry sorbet, all right, and then I will basically hand you a glass with the cocktail with the medicine."

"Yes," Grandma said, again, firm.

"I warn you, it tastes pretty gnarly. It's about two ounces, and the goal is to try to drink it as fast as possible without choking. Within a minute. And I do run a timer, OK? And I will kind of encourage you gently and I'll be right here next to you. You'll hand me the glass. I'll let you know that you're done, and I'll be waiting with more of the sorbet."

"OK."

"Because you can't see me, I'll just keep asking if you want some more, and you just tell me. If you don't want anymore, that's OK. You don't have to finish the whole . . . I got a whole jar of sorbet. I don't expect you to finish it. You just have as much as you need to get rid of the bad flavor. After you've had a few spoons of that, we'll let you back down, and I will expect you'll go to sleep within a few minutes. And then you will not wake up."

"Good," Grandma said.

We laughed.

The atmosphere was strangely festive. Laughing and smiling, jokes and lighthearted comments. To some degree, we were keeping a good face on for Grandma, but we were also happy to know that she would soon be beyond her suffering. The weight of the experience was on us all.

"Do you have questions, Bernice?" Dr. Fielder asked.

"Oh sure," she answered. "Because I'm so bright right now."

"What's that?"

"Because I'm so bright. No, I don't have any questions."

"And what about you guys?" Fielder turned to us.

There was silence for a moment, then I said, "How long?"

"After she falls asleep, the average, around the country, is about forty-five minutes. Up to two hours until she actually passes. But she will be fast asleep. Yeah, it's really hard to predict. I've had people pass within ten minutes. I have people—I always warn people there is the possibility. I mean, they're on record. The longest on record is nineteen hours."

"Wow," I said, almost under my breath.

"But that patient never woke up in the process. I don't think that's going to be the case, OK? But we never know."

"OK," I said.

Dr. Fielder picked up his bag, "So, Bernice? I'm going to go get ready now. I'll be right back."

"Yes," she answered.

In one hundred trillion years, the last star will have been born. Soon after, the last star will go out. Darkness and cold will seep in like a cosmic draft. Light and warmth will flicker as galaxies filled with dwarf stars and black holes collide and release energy, but soon those will wink out like candles during a power outage that never ends.

And one day (though it will be beyond any conception of "day" and "night," for both we ourselves and our solar system will have long since ceased to exist), approximately one hundred quintillion years in our future, entropy will reach its maximum point. Energy, such as it is by this point, will now be evenly spread throughout the universe, and no new sources will arise. Then entropy will decrease—fewer and fewer combinations will be possible as energy fades. Everything has become potential, but soon after, nothing will be anything at all.

In one googol years—that is, a 1 followed by 100 zeroes—the last bits of heat and energy will be gone.

While Dr. Fielder was in the other room, we tended to Grandma, rubbing her back, adjusting the pillows. Asking her about the temperature. Grandma, exhausted now, barely communicated with us. She was in pain and very, very tired.

Dr. Fielder soon returned with the promised sorbet. My mother perked up at the sight of the sorbet container and said, "Oh, you're getting all the bells and whistles, Bernice! This is no Jonestown!"

"True," I said. "He didn't bring enough for everyone."

Gallows humor didn't exactly abound, but it flitted in and out of the conversation as the morning progressed.

My uncle now spooned the sorbet into Grandma's mouth, slowly. "That's good," she said.

Dr. Fielder produced the medication itself, a chalky white substance in a clear cup. He gave grandma a straw. "Now put this in your mouth and drink it down as fast as you can. And when you're done, you can have more sorbet to get rid of that awful taste."

"But you have to earn it," I added, unable to stop myself. My sense of humor is often a shield against negative emotions. That day it served me well.

Grandma took her first sip, then paused and said one word. "Yuck." A few more moments passed and then she was done. Bruce gave her more sorbet.

"As much as you want of that, it's all yours," Dr. Fielder said. "If you want more, just open up your mouth, like a birdie."

We were all quiet now as she ate a few more spoonfuls.

"How do you feel?" I asked.

"I don't know," she murmured.

"You want to lie down?" Dr. Fielder asked. "Let's get you lying down now."

It was a team effort to help her lie back down. My hand on hers, the loose, fragile skin warm as I lowered her down. She was quiet now, the sedatives doing their work.

"Safe travels," Dr. Fielder said.

"Say hello to everyone!" my mother added.

She coughed, then groaned, then asked for her legs to be straightened out.

"Is the pillow comfortable?" Bruce asked.

"Yes," she answered, her voice small and fading.

Bruce held her hand. I kissed her head.

She fell asleep.

"And to let you guys know," Dr. Fielder said, "it's probably going to look like she's passed. And she may even turn blue. But then in a few minutes she'll start breathing again. Probably in about nine or ten minutes. That's very normal."

"OK," we said.

"And boy, she drank that like a champ," he said.

"She knew what she was about," my wife said. "She was ready."

And so we waited. My mother tucked her bedclothes. My wife now held her hand. We made small talk about how quickly she had fallen asleep. How effective the medication seemed to be. How many deaths the doctor had attended.

Then she breathed loudly, a sound like a snore. And was quiet again.

Minutes passed. The conversation continued. Then lulled. Then started again, then turned to laughter, almost like a holiday. Dr. Fielder said this wasn't unusual, that some families had music and cocktails. That some were somber, that everyone had a different way of facing the exit of their loved one.

"Her fingers are cold," my mother announced.

Dr. Fielder applied his stethoscope. She was still. "She has moved on. Nine fifty a.m. Nineteen minutes after taking the medicine."

"Good job, Bernice," my mother said.

A googol years in the future, the universe is dark, cold, and quiet.

Or is it? The end of the universe is far beyond our ability to comprehend, and infinite variables cloud our predictions. We give our lack of understanding names that reflect our unknowing: dark matter, dark energy, our equations confounded when we try to figure out, for instance, why the universe seems to be accelerating in its expansion or the strange noise in background radiation. And the totality of our ignorance? Scientists call it "cosmic uncertainty."

So, dark, cold, and quiet. Or something else? A change in state as energy reaches its end? A path forward through the darkness?

We don't know. We may never know. We just hope for the best.

While you're alive and able—be good.

NUCLEAR FAMILY

Acknowledgments

Courtney, of course, my partner in all things.

My mother and sister, who lived through it with me. My grandmother, for her life and mine. All the Bannermans, living and dead. Marie Landau and Brenton Woodward for rescuing the manuscript when it looked like it was doomed to languish forgotten in a desk until all the uranium in the universe turned to lead. Mike, Jenn, Lisa, Lauren, and the other Dirt City Writers. Dorothy Vanderford, for giving me a peak at Oppenheimerhood. My teachers and mentors, Greg Martin, Dana Levin, V. B. Price, and Justin St. Germain.

Thank you.